FAITH OF OUR FATHERS

Jackson, Charles L. *Faith of Our Fathers: A Study of the Nicene Creed.*
Copyright © 2007 L. Charles Jackson.

Published by Canon Press, P.O. Box 8729, Moscow, ID 83843
1-800-488-2034 | www.canonpress.com
Printed in the United States of America.
Cover design by David Dalbey.

07 08 09 10 11 12   9 8 7 6 5 4 3 2 1

Library of Congress Cataloging-in-Publication Data

Jackson, L. Charles.
  Faith of our fathers : a popular study of the Nicene Creed / L. Charles
Jackson.
    p. cm.
  Includes bibliographical references.
  ISBN-13: 978-1-59128-043-9 (pbk.)
  ISBN-10: 1-59128-043-5 (pbk.)
  1. Nicene Creed. I. Title.

  BT999.J33 2007
  238'.142--dc22

                                              2007002710

FAITH
OF OUR
FATHERS

A Study of the Nicene Creed

L. CHARLES JACKSON

CANON
PRESS
Moscow, Idaho

The Nicene Creed

We believe in one God, the Father, the Almighty, maker of heaven and earth, of all that is, seen and unseen.

We believe in one Lord, Jesus Christ, the only Son of God, eternally begotten of the Father, God from God, Light from Light, true God from true God, begotten, not made, of one Being with the Father; through Him all things were made.

For us and for our salvation He came down from heaven, was incarnate of the Holy Spirit and the Virgin Mary and became truly human. For our sake He was crucified under Pontius Pilate; He suffered death and was buried. On the third day He rose again in accordance with the Scriptures; He ascended into heaven and is seated at the right hand of the Father. He will come again in glory to judge the living and the dead, and His kingdom will have no end.

We believe in the Holy Spirit, the Lord, the giver of life, who proceeds from the Father and the Son, who with the Father and the Son is worshipped and glorified, who has spoken through the prophets.

We believe in one holy, catholic, and apostolic Church. We acknowledge one baptism for the forgiveness of sins.

We look for the resurrection of the dead, and the life of the world to come. Amen.

Translation: The English Language Liturgical Consultation

Contents

1   "No Creed but Christ"?

> If one word could sum up the current theological situation, it would be amnesia. The real problem with amnesia, of course, is that not only does the patient forget his loved ones and friends, but he no longer remembers who he is. Too many within church leadership today seem to have forgotten that the building of a foundational Christian identity is based upon that which the church has received, preserved, and carefully transmitted to each generation of believers.[1]

What do you believe? A confident young man, attempting to sound neutral and levelheaded, might remark, "No creed but Christ: that's my confession of faith." He continues, "I don't like all these divisive doctrinal questions. They just create a negative and intolerant religious environment."

How quickly and easily this comment rolls off the lips of so many people! You would think that rattling off this mantra relieves a person of all the entanglements of doctrinal controversy. After all, doesn't everyone know that "doctrine divides"? This seems to be the conventional wisdom of the day. People today are desperate to escape the snares of dogma, denominations, and other negative religiously entangling controversies. They believe that the barnacles of doctrinal controversy have scarred the church so badly that we should avoid dogma and doctrine like some kind of a medieval plague.

---

1. D.H. Williams, *Retrieving the Tradition and Renewing Evangelicalism: A Primer for Suspicious Protestants* (Grand Rapids: Eerdmans, 1999), 9.

This provokes a very important question: would avoiding creeds and confessions really liberate us from our problems or clear away the confusion? When you begin to tackle this question, an irony emerges. When someone is asked the most basic questions about Jesus Christ, they immediately begin to articulate a creedal statement. What do you believe about Jesus? Was He really God? Was He fully God or was He only partly divine? I thought He was the Son of God and not God from all eternity. How does this make any sense? How could He be both God and man? How could He exist in one person with two distinct natures? On one level these questions are quiet simple. Yet, on another level these are the questions that drive us to the very foundations of our faith. What do you believe about Jesus? A creed of course helps to provide answers to these simple questions.

A creed, in fact, is the result of answering these questions. Yes, any attempt to answer these questions results in a creed even if it is only a poorly worded or false one. Creeds, therefore, are unavoidable. This is too central to miss; creeds are unavoidable. The word *creed* comes from the Latin *credo,* meaning "I believe." Any attempt to confess what one believes is a creed. Saying "no creed but Christ" is just as much a creed as a written statement is a creed. You should see the self-contradictory problem with saying "no creed but Christ." Even though it is short and rather ill-conceived it is nonetheless a confession or creed. Hence, rather than liberating themselves from the snares of creeds, those who say this have actually entangled themselves in a poorly conceived one.

The Scriptures say in James 2:19, "You believe that there is one God. You do well. Even the demons believe—and tremble! It is never enough to say that you "believe." The real question remains: *what* do you believe about Jesus? Reality has a way of foisting this upon us. When you consider that Islam, Judaism, Mormonism, and a whole host of other religions all acknowledge a belief in Jesus, it should be obvious that affirming a belief in Jesus is simply not enough.

In order to be organized and meaningful, even a local community club develops some kind of guidelines to distinguish who is a member and who is not. At this point, confessions of faith become not only necessary but also vital to the well-being of the church. Creeds protect us from error and guide us in truth. Knowing a creed can help to distinguish a Muslim from a Christian. Most reasonable people would affirm that this is helpful. Furthermore, if you assume Christianity to be true, it is not an exaggeration to say that knowing a creed may make the difference between heaven and hell.

The foregoing examples should make it clear that creeds have always been a necessary and obvious part of being a follower of Christ. As one great historian of the creeds, Philip Schaff, says,

> In a certain sense it may be said that the Christian Church has never been without a creed (*Ecclesia sine symbolis nulla*). The baptismal formula and the words of institution of the Lord's Supper are creeds; these and the confession of Peter antedate even the birth of the Christian Church on the day of Pentecost. The Creed is indeed not founded on symbols, but on Christ; not on any words of man, but on the word of God; yet it is founded on Christ as confessed by men.[2]

As Schaff notes, the concept of confessing God by means of a creed was not the invention of the Christian Church. Indeed, some have even argued that God Himself required the ancient Jews to confess him by means of a creed called the *shema*. The shema is a kind of primal creed found in Deuteronomy 6:4: "Hear, O Israel: the Lord our God the Lord is one." God required this creed and Jesus Himself used it to answer various people when He was confronted with basic questions.[3]

Creeds are not only necessary; they are also helpful. Creeds help us answer very old and very difficult questions. Too many

2. Philip Schaff, *The Creeds of Christendom: With a History and Critical Notes,* Vol. I: The History of Creeds (Baker Grand Rapids: Baker, 1990 [1931]), 5.

3. See Jaroslav Pelikan, *Credo: Historical and Theological Guide to Creeds and Confessions of Faith in the Christian Tradition* (Yale Univ. Press, 2003), 374.

people today try to answer these questions as if they were the first person to face the issue. The sad truth is that they are like the frustrated little boy who wonders how he can make one of his toys move faster. He begins to wonder if he could stop dragging his toy along the ground and make it move more smoothly. He asks himself, "What would help my toys move faster and what would it look like? What shape would it take? How could things move faster than being dragged on the ground? The agonizing problem seems laughable to those of us who desperately want the little fellow to take a look at the wheels on his father's car. Wouldn't that help? Creeds help us like this. They keep us from trying to reinvent the wheel.

The ancient creeds of the church are God's gift to us; they are not doctrinal entanglements. Ironically, they are not the cause of doctrinal controversy; they are the answer to it. We should be happy to know that the ancient creeds of the church can liberate us from the frustrations of doctrinal controversy. They ease the burden of reinventing the wheel and lift us onto the shoulders of men who have gone before us. This is a great benefit. This gives us a very good advantage. For instance, instead of trying to create a wheel, we can move on to other things. We can, for example, work on fine-tuning the engine or make the interior more comfortable.

Creeds are like lights in a dark world. There is always a lot of theological work to be done, but it is easier to do the work in the light rather than in the dark. We don't need to turn off the lights and grope around in the darkness. Creeds can act like lights in dark times. In the middle of a difficult controversy, creeds can help to clear away the confusion and provide us with guidance. In certain settings, groping in the dark can be quite dangerous. Thus, to ignore the light and guidance of creeds would be folly and arrogance.

I have heard some people say that they don't want to depend on other people for truth. They would prefer to work it out on their own. "All I need," they say, "is Jesus and my Bible." They act as if depending on the work of others diminishes independence of thought. This, however, is not the Christian approach to life. Indeed, it is nothing more than arrogance cloaked in false piety.

Looking to the past reveals both wisdom and humility. We should humbly look to the past for help and we should not be embarrassed to do so. It is as obvious as asking your parents a question about something that you know they have already confronted and overcome. Wouldn't a wise son ask his father for help? Men who have lived before us are just as much our parents in the faith as those who live today. This is partly why the men of the ancient church are called the "fathers." The Bible tells us to honor our fathers. It is a sign of due and proper humility to ask people who already know the answers rather than to tackle the problem all on our own.

It is not a sign of humility to rely solely on yourself. To the contrary, it reeks of arrogance. Charles Spurgeon says the following:

> You are not such wiseacres as to think or say that you can expound the Scripture without the assistance from the works of divine and learned men who have labored before you in the field of exposition. . . . It seems odd that certain men who talk so much of what the Holy Spirit reveals to themselves, should think so little of what he has revealed to others.[4]

Creeds not only provide us with help, guidance, and humility—they are also an excellent witness to a needy world. In the Great Commission in Matthew 28, Christ commands Christians to make disciples, baptizing them and teaching them all that He commanded them. Creeds help us teach others the faith. Indeed, Christ also tells His followers in Matthew 10:32 to "confess" him before men. Paul says the same thing in Romans 10:9: "If you will confess with your mouth the Lord Jesus Christ and believe in your heart that God has raised him from the dead, you shall be saved."

---

4. Charles H. Spurgeon, *Commenting and Commentaries,* Lecture 1.

This means that creeds can be a useful part of our liturgy. As we confess our God, we also experience the blessing of doing so with others who share this faith with us. Thus too we corporately confess our faith to the watching world. Creeds assist us to worship in a way that is decent and orderly. What a blessing to our children who grow up hearing this truth over and over again—they are more likely to remember and believe it. Philip Schaff reminds us,

> There is an express duty, when we are received into the membership of the Christian Church, and on every proper occasion, to profess the faith within us, to make ourselves known as followers of Christ, and to lead others to him by the influence of our testimony.[5]

This express duty is running into conflict with popular notions about growing the church. There seems to be nothing less than an obsession to diminish doctrine so that the church can grow. After all, people may not agree with doctrine, and what really matters is that they just believe in Jesus. I hope you can see how this raises the obvious question, "*What* do you believe about Jesus?"

Are you really being sensitive to those who are "seeking" answers if you avoid "teaching them whatever Jesus has commanded you" as He says in the Great Commission? Is growing the church really the only thing that Jesus requires in the Great Commission? You may be able to grow a large congregation, but are you being faithful to the Great Commission, which requires "teaching" people what they must confess—or in other words, teaching them creeds? Jesus pushed Peter to this very point when He insisted that Peter answer the question, "Yes, but who do you say that I am?" Sooner or later, in this world or in the next, we will be responsible for how we answer this question.

While the whole world seems to be going insane over the notion of tolerance, Christians need to strive to make sense of

5. Schaff, *Creeds of Christendom*, 4.

the master's demands. We should not be afraid of taking the time to cultivate substance and excellence in how we confess our Lord. Creeds can even help us do this. Though directed to a somewhat different point, Alexis de Tocqueville's words are appropriate when he says,

> All who aspire to literary excellence in democratic nations ought frequently to refresh themselves at the springs of ancient literature; there is no more wholesome medicine for the mind. . . . I think that they have some special merits, admirably calculated to counterbalance our peculiar defects.[6]

Of course if we are either ignorant or arrogant, we won't admit that we have any "peculiar defects." Still, if this sage advice is true of the uninspired literature of antiquity, how much more aptly does it direct us to the creeds of our faith? Those of us who long for Christian excellence in a creedless and chaotic age must drink deeply from the refreshing springs of our ancient confessions. There is no more wholesome medicine to the soul. To ignore them would not only be arrogant, it would be tragic and deadly.

Creeds protect us from danger. If you were walking along a forest path, wouldn't you appreciate it if someone warned you of a dangerous animal further down the trail? If you were about to drive a car with no brakes, wouldn't you appreciate it if someone warned you? Creeds offer us this kind of a warning so we can avoid potential dangers. This is precisely why the Nicene Creed was written. It was forged in the heat of dangerous controversy.

The Council of Nicea was convened because of prevailing questions about the nature of the relationship between Jesus Christ and God the Father. These were no small questions. According to T. F. Torrance,

> The basic decision taken at Nicaea [sic] made it clear that the eternal relation between the Father and the Son in the

6. Alexis de Tocqueville, *Democracy in America,* vol. 2 (New York: Vintage Books, 1990), 62.

Godhead was regarded in the Church as the supreme truth upon which everything else in the Gospel depends. . . . Thus the very essence of the Gospel and the whole of the Christian faith depend on the centrality and primacy of the relation in being and agency between Jesus Christ and God the Father.[7]

When someone says they have "no creed but Christ," they may think it sounds tolerant and wise, but it is neither. It is not only unwise, but it is the height of arrogance and foolishness. Worse yet, it is not only personally foolish, it is dangerous to the whole Christian community. The question is never *if* you have a confession; the question is always *what* your confession is. This is where the Nicene Creed offers us light in the darkness and guidance in dangerous times.

Study Questions

1. Why do some people avoid creeds?
2. Why are creeds unavoidable?
3. What does the word *credo* mean?
4. Why isn't it enough to believe in one God?
5. Were creeds the invention of the church?
6. What Bible references speak of confessing the faith?
7. List several ways that creeds can help us.
8. How does using creeds express humility?
9. What was the main issue of the Council of Nicea?
10. Find some Bible passages not cited in the chapter that are relevant to these issues.

7. T. F. Torrance, *The Trinitarian Faith: The Evangelical Theology of the Ancient Catholic Church* (Edinburgh: T & T Clark, 1988), 3, 5.

2 A Corporate Confession

We believe . . .

In Greek, the first word of the Nicene Creed is the verb *pistuomen,* which means "we believe." While the Apostle's Creed begins with the words, "I believe," the Nicene Creed begins with the first person plural pronoun: "*We* believe." This strikes some people as a distinctive and an improper use of the first person plural. Why did the fathers begin with the pronoun *we?* After all, isn't it more personal to speak of what *I* believe as an individual Christian rather than what *we* believe as Christians?

Though some in the Middle Ages proposed that the apostles themselves created the Apostle's Creed, it was not a creed formulated officially in the courts or councils of the church. This may partially account for the first person singular pronoun of the apostle's creed. However, there is a wealth of wisdom in the powerful little word *we.*

As the church's first "official" ecumenical creed, the Nicene Creed was not the expression of an individual, but of the corporate body of Christ; the church. In this sense, both historically and doctrinally the creed reflects something pointedly Christian regarding the corporate character of the faith. There is an important unifying and communal character to the first word of the Nicene Creed.

The creed expresses the Christian belief that the faith we possess is "our" faith, not primarily "my" faith. The faith that we believe as Christians is the faith given to us from our Father in heaven. Hence, there is a unity and diversity properly acknowledged in the first word of the creed. All those who would follow after Christ must join with others who also believe what Christ requires us to believe. There is one God who is gathering unto Himself a people, the church. This one God is gathering His people together in the truth that He has given to His people collectively or corporately.

As such the creed establishes that Christianity is most definitely not an individualistic religion. It is personal, yes, but not individualistic. Individualism creates splintering, centrifugal forces, which cause nations, churches and families to fly wildly apart. Christianity, on the other hand, has always been a vital force for social unity and cultural coherence. Hence, the creed starts with an antidote to individualism using the potent phrase "We believe."

The Nicene Creed is not something an individual believes in isolation from the church. The authors of the creed did not believe they were expressing the collected thoughts of isolated individuals. No, they truly believed that the creed expressed quite literally the God-breathed faith of the Scriptures as given to the church. This is why they referred to the creed as expressing "the divine and apostolic faith."[1]

The truth of this creed is not something new nor is it something optional. It is simply what Christians believe. If one is a Christian, then this is the faith that one must confess. It is also the faith one shares with others as members of this one body.

Individuals are not free to modify, restructure, or change the faith in order to suit their individual tastes. This is the objective faith to which each individual must submit and to which each individual must subscribe as that which joins all those who follow Christ.

This is radically different from the pervasive individualism of our times. Because he or she tends to define the ultimate meaning of life entirely in terms of "individual" choice, the individualist is quite uncomfortable with the corporate or cov-

---

1. T. F. Torrance, *The Trinitarian Faith*, 14.

enantal aspect of Christianity. The "we" statement of the creed unifies individuals and strikes an aggressive pose against individualism, which by definition isolates rather than unifies.

Alexis de Tocqueville noted the isolating tendencies of individualism in his insightful work *Democracy in America*:

> Individualism is a calm and considered feeling which disposes each citizen to isolate himself from the mass of his fellows and withdraw into the circle of family and friends; with this little society formed to his tastes, he gladly leaves the greater society to look after itself. . . . They form the habit of thinking of themselves in isolation and imagine that their whole destiny is in their hands. . . . Each man is forever thrown back on himself alone, and there is a danger that he may be shut up in the solitude of his own heart. [2]

De Tocqueville points us to the isolation that God declared "not good" in the Garden of Eden. If expressing oneself, as a human being is an individual issue, then God's design for men must have been mistaken. God deliberately created Adam first so He could establish several things, not the least of which was the fact of Adam's solitary existence prior to Eve's creation. God said, "It is not good for man to be alone." Isolation and individualism countermands God's creation design. Consequently, individualism creates the opposite of what it pretends to offer. Rather than providing the personal fulfillment of which it falsely boasts, it actually yields chaos, insecurity and frustration. It is precisely this kind of chaos and frustration for which Christianity provides the cure.

We cannot fall prey to the false division between what is individual and what is personal. We are social creatures. We can, therefore, believe something personally while sharing this personal belief with others. Individualism violates a veritable maxim of the faith, as one preacher, Benjamin Morgan Palmer, notes:

2. De Tocqueville, *Democracy in America*.

That man, endowed with a social nature, cannot attain the perfection which is possible to him, in the privacy and insulation of his own being. . . . [I]t is not true that religion contemplates man as an insulated being. On the contrary, it penetrates every faculty of his complex nature, and pervades every relation in which he stands. As the moon's motion round the earth does not impede the common and wider motion of both around the sun, so neither does the connection between God and the conscience become less intimate, when the worshipper lifts his voice in the great congregation, than when he breathes his prayer in the whispers of the closet.[3]

Many people assume as a matter of fact that individualism is the only acceptable approach to personal fulfillment. With the advent of this way of thinking the ideas and practices that were once standard elements of social cohesion have flown apart. This is contrary to the created order and hence to God's design. Consequently, individualism cannot provide the happiness it pretends to furnish.

Individualism breeds isolation and selfishness, while Christianity demands the opposite. The "we" of Christianity requires unity and it demands a concern for others. The Christian must live for the glory of God and the welfare of his neighbor. Sin disrupted this original design, but Christ has come to repair the ruins of our fallen parents.

Thus the "we" of the creed's opening statement not only demands unity, but also implies obligation and responsibility to one's neighbor. Individualism ranks as perhaps the most petulant problem of modern and postmodern times. Individualism creates impulses of selfish disregard for other people. This isn't merely the raving of "religious" leaders. This is something that most thoughtful observers are noting. Political leaders, educa-

---

3. Benjamin Morgan Palmer, "The Warrant and Nature of Public Worship," a sermon preached on 9 October 1853 in Columbia, South Carolina. Reproduced online at <www.swrb.com/newslett/actualNLs/publwors.htm>.

tors, and sociologists of all stripes recognize the harmful, isolating forces of individualism. One study notes,

> If the entire social world is made up of individuals, each endowed with the right to be free of others' demands, it becomes hard to forge bonds of attachment to or cooperation with, other people, since such bonds would imply obligations that necessarily impinge on one's freedom.[4]

It is precisely this kind of obligation that Christianity demands. Christ came not to be served, but to serve. This He demands of His followers as well:

> Let nothing be done through selfish ambition or conceit, but in lowliness of mind let each esteem others better than himself. Let each of you look out not only for his own interests, but also for the interests of others. Let this mind be in you which was also in Christ Jesus, who . . . made Himself of no reputation, taking the form of a bondservant, and coming in the likeness of men. And being found in appearance as a man, He humbled Himself and became obedient to the point of death, even the death of the cross. (Phil. 2:3–8)

Jesus came to save sinners; He came to be a servant to the needy. Of the multiple teachings of Christianity one basic principle is the call to live an "others-oriented" existence. Jesus is our great example, and hence, the creed says, He "for us and for our salvation came down from heaven and became man." Jesus became a human being so that He could save His people; He loved needy sinners and it follows necessarily that those who love him must also serve others as well.

While some people and some cultures nourish individualism as a virtue, Christianity assaults it as a curse. The Nicene formula helps us to appreciate that Christianity in its most basic form attacks individualism like antibodies attack germs in the body. The incarnation destroys individualism, which is why

---

4. Robert N. Bellah, et. al, eds., *Habits of the Heart: Individualism and Commitment in American Life* (New York: Harper & Row), 23.

our first ecumenical creed at Nicea begins with the profoundly important pronoun *we*. Christianity is corporate and demands living in selfless community after the pattern of and under the person of Jesus Christ. This and much more is unleashed in the simple but staggeringly potent opening phrase of the Nicene Creed: "We believe."

STUDY QUESTIONS

1. How does the Nicene Creed's introduction differ from that of the Apostle's Creed?
2. What could account for this difference?
3. What is individualism?
4. Explain why Christianity is not individualistic.
5. Are individuals free to modify or change Christian beliefs?
6. How does individualism tend to isolate rather than unite?
7. Is there a necessary contrast between something personal and something corporate?
8. Can something be corporate and personal at the same time?
9. How is individualism contrary to divine design?
10. According to the author, what does the "we" of Christianity imply?
11. How does Jesus' example help us?
12. Find some Bible passages not cited in the chapter that are relevant to these issues.

3 Faith and Godliness

We believe . . .

New trends for church growth or the establishment of "seeker sensitive" settings have replaced the church's corporate memory for directing ecclesial policies and theological education. . . . And all the while, the issue of determining Christian identity has lost its way in the mists of emotionally charged and professionally orchestrated worship. It is not that Christians are purposely ignoring Paul's final words to Timothy, "preserve the pattern of sound teaching . . . guard the good deposit that was entrusted to you," it is that they are no longer sure what the "deposit" consists of, or where it can be found. In some cases, finding this "deposit" does not matter anymore.[1]

Before we move on to other sections, we will pause just briefly again for another look at the first word of the creed. The Greek word meaning "we believe" has a bit more depth to it than you might first imagine. The word indicates much more than mere intellectual assent. It can even be translated "I trust" or "I have faith." In the first word of the creed we find that faith and godliness are intimately connected. Athanasius says,

> Faith and godliness are connected and are sisters: he who believes in God is not cut off from godliness, and he who has godliness really believes.[2]

1. D.H. Williams, *Retrieving the Tradition and Renewing Evangelicalism: A Primer for Suspicious Protestants*, (Grand Rapids: Eerdmans, 1999), 10.
2. Quoted in Torrance, *Trinitarian Faith,* 43.

For some reason there are many Christians who propagate the idea that doctrine can somehow be separated from life. Some people act as if there can be a radical separation between what one "believes" and how one "lives." The Nicene Creed doesn't allow for such a separation. The original word for "we believe" won't allow for such a separation.

Modern and postmodern culture has nurtured a false sense of separation between what one says and what one does. In the 1990s Americans in particular suffered greatly as a culture because of the separation between words and life. This treachery came from the highest levels of political and corporate leadership. Even one of presidents of the United States lied under oath and then quibbled over the definition of the word *is*.

Leaders seemed to wink at perjury as long as it was used to cover over a political scandal and as long as they didn't get caught. However, one cannot separate words from actions without tragic results. If someone can say one thing and then do another thing, then social order itself is disturbed. Not too long after the deeply divisive political scandals in America, many corporations cooked their accounting books in order to appear more profitable. Corporate leaders attempted to act as if they could separate words from actions, but again the bankruptcies that resulted wrought tragic consequences for the average investor. Most certainly this kind of slippery and elusive approach to words and their meanings has contributed to a low view of making a confession of faith that actually binds one's actions. Nevertheless, words are always connected to actions even if in the case of a liar his words betray him and undermine trust. Words and actions are always connected. This was something foundational to the fathers at Nicea.

"We believe" demands more than a mere intellectual set of ideas. This word's relationship to the believer runs far deeper than simply an abstract set of doctrines for the brain. In other words, you could even loosely translate the first part of the creed as saying, "We *trust* in one God the Father Almighty, Maker of heaven and earth, and of all things visible and invisible." This is not merely something intellectual.

According to the creed, there can be no separation or division between what one believes and how one lives. To believe is to trust and to trust is to believe. To believe is to follow. We follow the one God the Father Almighty, who is the maker of all things. This is the one and only God for whom we live and for whom we die. To believe is to live. The creed offers faith and godliness as an inseparable package.

Just as the Father and the Son are inseparable, so faith cannot be separated from godly living. Indeed, well-known theologian T. F. Torrance says,

> An outstanding mark of the Nicene approach was its association of faith with "piety" or "godliness," that is with a mode of worship, behavior and thought that was devout and worthy of God the Father and the Son and the Holy Spirit.[3]

Faith and godliness cannot possibly be separated because the Faith is not subjectively grounded in human reason or human emotion. The Faith as objectively revealed from God is grounded in God Himself. This is why the way we live can't be separated from what—or in this case, from the *one*—in whom we believe.

When we confess our belief in God the Father, the Son, and the Holy Spirit we are also offering praise and worship to God, which makes the Nicene Creed particularly well suited for worship. Godliness and theology are never separated, and so to confess Christ is to worship him as well. The Nicene Creed thus offers an obviously practical tool for liturgy. Indeed, this is one of the many reasons why the Nicene Creed is almost universally used in a wide variety of Christian traditions. The Nicene Creed is used in a bewildering array of worship services

3. Torrance, *The Trinitarian Faith,* 17.

across the world: Roman Catholic, Greek Orthodox,[4] and a number of Protestant traditions confess their faith Sunday by Sunday using it.

Historically, Christians have recognized this foundational aspect of the creed. Because the creed is so basic, it serves the whole Christian world beautifully. It offers the most funda- mental ideas that are common to the gospel message regardless of culture, tradition, or background. This is the most basic confession of Christianity, which is not grounded in any hu- man source, but in God's revelation of Himself to us.

The creed thus serves us as a tool for worship and also as a tool for evangelism. This is after all not just a group of ideas, but the gospel. If one knows the creed, then one is capable of spreading the good news that the creed asserts. While it is cer- tainly not merely a naked set of ideas, it is still an objective set of ideas as well. This is not a dilemma. It is not an "either/or," but it is a "both/and." Children who grow up confessing this creed will also grow up knowing the gospel message. What a blessing for our children!

The creed, then, in a quite astounding sense, is liturgical and evangelical at the same time. It helps us to worship our God as it offers the gospel message to the needy world. In cor- porate, public worship, the church confesses and makes known the faith. This would correspond well with Paul's statements in Ephesians 3:10: ". . . to the intent that now the manifold wisdom of God might be made known by the church to the principalities and powers in the heavenly places."

We should use this blessed gift of providence for our chil- dren as a guide for worship and as an evangelical blessing to the world. The gospel message is not a set of ideas, but a gift of grace that God desires us to pass on to all men. Consequently, there is hope in this confession. We confess the hope of Christ to each other, to our children, and to the watching world. If Paul's words connect here, we also confess it to the very angels

---

4. The Greek Church uses the original Nicene formulation of A.D. 325 without the *filioque* addition of a later council.

in heaven. Indeed this is the confession in which lies the only true hope for fallen, sinful humanity. It is also the confession in which the glory of the riches of God's grace unfolds the mystery of the gospel. In our father Adam all die, but in Christ all will be made alive.

The fathers of Nicea never thought they were merely formulating a really helpful intellectual guide. From their writings it appears that they couldn't have conceived of the creed as a bare statement of doctrinal ideas. Promoting the truth was the same as promoting godliness, and thus promoting the hope of Christ. This was no abstract formula; this was not an academic exercise; this is the faith. This is what must be believed and this is what must be lived; faith and godliness melded inextricably together. There can be no separation because they are one and the same. Torrance captures this:

> The more truly God is known in accordance with His nature, the more godliness is advanced, and the more godliness is advanced the more likely we are to know God in a godly way that is worthy of His nature as God. Generally speaking, then, the aim is to get as near the truth as possible and to shape our belief according to the rule of godliness. Thus godliness and the rule of truth became operational equivalents.[5]

STUDY QUESTIONS
1. Give two other words that could be translated from the Greek word for "believe."
2. If you cannot separate what you believe from how you live, then can you separate doctrine from life?
3. Why can't our words and actions ever be separated?
4. Why can't faith and godliness ever be separated?
5. How does the creed offer a practical tool for worship?
6. How does the creed offer a practical tool for evangelism?
7. Find some Bible passages not cited in the chapter that are relevant to these issues.

5. Torrance, *Trinitarian Faith,* 38.

4 — Access to the Father

We believe in one God, the Father Almighty . . .

The Council of Nicea could have opened the creed with the bare assertion that God is the "creator." This is certainly true. The bishops could have started with an assertion that God is the only independent being. They could have simply declared that we believe in "God almighty." A variety of possible expressions could have opened the creed. Indeed, they could have selected a popular title from classical culture, which refers to the divine being as the "unmoved mover." Yet, they began with God as Father. Why? Why didn't the patriarchs of our faith designate God as the "unmoved mover"?

Choosing this title at the opening of the creed reveals an important theological commitment in Christianity: human beings cannot know God unless He reveals Himself to them. One could restate this by saying, "God can't be known unless He makes Himself known." This is a fundamental plank in the theology that emerges from Nicea. This also explains why the Nicene Creed begins with the definition of God as "Father."

Since understanding God depends on His revelation of Himself to us, and since the focus of God's revelation to man is Jesus, God is best known as "Father." Indeed, Jesus is the focus and sum of the entire revelation of God to His people. All things from Genesis to Revelation point in some fashion to the person and work of Jesus.

The incarnation of the Son is not only the focus of the Bible, but it is the central focus of human history as well. The coming of Jesus is referred to in the Bible as the "fullness of the times"

(Eph. 1:10; Gal. 4:4). All of history from the beginning of time to the consummation of all things finds its meaning in God's revelation of Himself in the person of Jesus. This brought the fledgling faith into sharp and radical contrast with the classical world.

The gods of the Greeks and the Romans were Zeus and his cadre of Olympian divines were really nothing more than exaggerated humans who also were associated with the impersonal forces of fate that govern history. They were bigger, stronger, and lived forever, but they were essentially the projection of humanity onto divinity. According to T. F. Torrance, this became a fundamental distinction of Christianity from its classical context:

> When the Christian Gospel was proclaimed in that context, very quickly a sharp conflict emerged between Hellenistic and Hebraic patterns of thought, between a mythological way of thinking from a center in the human mind and a theological way of thinking from a center in God. In particular, the biblical teaching about God's providential and saving activity in history, and the Christian message of incarnation and redemption in space and time . . . [1]

If mythology is the projection of human thoughts and ideals onto divinity, then theology is fundamentally different. Rather than thoughts which originate in the minds of human beings, Christianity takes its thoughts from the mind of God. The word *theology* is the combination of two Greek words, *theos* (God) and *logos* (word). Christians know God because He has revealed Himself to them in His Son, whom the apostle John calls the *logos*, the "word" from God (Jn. 1:1ff). Therefore, as the Nicene fathers opened the creed, they focused primarily on the relationship between the Father and Son. This was the relationship which, according to biblical revelation, takes primacy as it regards the gospel.

---

1. Torrance, *Trinitarian Faith*, 47.

"All things have been delivered to Me by My Father, and no one knows who the Son is except the Father, and who the Father is except the Son, and the one to whom the Son wills to reveal Him." Then He turned to His disciples and said privately, "Blessed are the eyes which see the things you see . . ." (Lk. 10:22–23)

We must remember that the creed as we have duly noted was not merely an intellectual formula; it was a statement of faith and worship. Note Athanasius' insights: "It would be more godly and true to signify God from the Son and call him Father, than to name God from His works alone and call him 'Unoriginate.'"[2]

Heaven speaks down to earth and creatures are to look up and listen, responding with worship. This is theological thinking, which is thinking centered upon the ultimate revelation of God from heaven—Jesus Christ the Son of the living God. This is, after all, the way Peter confessed Jesus in Matthew 16:15–17:

He said to them, "But who do you say that I am?" Simon Peter answered and said, "You are the Christ, the Son of the living God." Jesus answered and said to him, "Blessed are you, Simon Bar-Jonah, for flesh and blood has not revealed this to you, but My Father who is in heaven."

Jesus tells us that such a confession originates in heaven and is a revelation of the Father in heaven to His humble followers here on earth. This is the opposite of mythology. As such it requires not only recognition of certain facts, but humility to God's words from heaven. Torrance again: "Piety and truth, godliness and accuracy, belong inseparably together in authentic knowledge of God through Jesus Christ His Son."[3]

We are pointed once again to piety or godliness in the confession. For centuries, mythology and mythological patterns of thinking dominated the classical world of the Greeks and

---

2. Athanasius, qtd. in ibid., 49.
3. Torrance, *Trinitarian Faith*, 49.

Romans. Christianity boldly challenged this way of thinking and not only demanded a change of thought, but required a posture of worship.

As creatures, neither the human mind nor the human soul is the origin of our knowledge of God. We are to humble ourselves to the revelation of God Himself to us. The creed challenged the classical world in many ways. According to Torrance, this kind of theological thinking began to point the western world to a more precise and objective approach to knowledge in general.

If one sought to know God, then one needed to investigate Him precisely as He reveals Himself. That is, He must be known in accordance with His own nature and attributes. You are not allowed to make up your own ideas. You are not allowed to project your own thoughts onto God. Hence, you are forced into a precise way of thinking that we oftentimes associate with scientific inquiry.

> Precise, scientific knowledge was held to result from inquiry strictly in accordance with the nature of the reality being investigated that is, knowledge of it reached under the constraint of what it actually and essentially is in itself, and not according to arbitrary convention. To know things in this way, strictly in accordance with their nature, is to know them in accordance with their truth or reality. And thus to think and speak truly of them. That is the only way to reach real, exact or scientific knowledge in any field of inquiry, through the faithful assent of the mind to the compelling or "cataleptic" claims of reality upon it.[4]

The fathers spoke of God under the constraints of His own distinctive nature as this nature is revealed in the person and work of Jesus. Knowing something like this is taking what many would call a "scientific" approach to knowledge. Certainly God required this kind of precision and attention to detail. One can see, however, the benefits of such an approach to knowledge.

4. Torrance, *Trinitarian Faith*, 51.

If this is true of God, it is also true of other things. Hence, the western conception of scientific truth and knowledge had a theological foundation.

Scientific knowledge, however, was hardly the primary concern of the fathers. Their major concern was the gospel. They wanted to confess the good news of God's love for sinners. This evangelical concern was paramount to their entitling God as Father.

It was a great a blessing to the classical world to hear that the true God of history was not only personal but all-loving and all-caring. The classical gods had worked in the world as faraway, inscrutable agents who affected history for a variety of petty reasons. It was a blessing in contrast for the gospel to break into this context. All things in history pointed to the coming of Jesus, and all things since His resurrection and ascension are moving to the consummation of all things in Christ. History has meaning and purpose in the loving work of Jesus Christ.

The God of Christianity is the personal God of history who loves sinners enough to send His only Son into time and space to redeem needy people. This is certainly not a blessing limited to the classical world. This is the universal need of all people in all places and at all times.

We approach God as Father and not simply as the impersonal, uncreated being. This leads us to worship him more deeply. His fatherhood as expressed in the person of Jesus Christ is personal, loving and kind. The creed, then, helps us to worship as much as it helps us to articulate a formal idea. We come to our God as our Father. What a warm and inviting image of God! God is not impersonal; He is a Father known primarily through His Son Jesus.

Indeed, since God gave us His only Son, we are drawn to Him not merely as our Creator, but as the compassionate Father. This is the God who gave His only Son. The well-known verse from John 3:16 is appropriate: "For God so loved the world that He gave His only begotten Son, that whoever believes in Him should not perish but have everlasting life. For

God did not send His Son into the world to condemn the world, but that the world through Him might be saved."

Thus, when we pray to God as Father we are drawn to him warmly as a child comes to his earthly father. We have access to God as Father through Jesus Christ alone. We hope in Him and we worship Him. As we come in the name of Jesus His Son, we expect the kind of reception a son gets from his earthly father. See Luke 11:11–13:

> If a son asks for bread from any father among you, will he give him a stone? Or if he asks for a fish, will he give him a serpent instead of a fish? Or if he asks for an egg, will he offer him a scorpion? If you then, being evil, know how to give good gifts to your children, how much more will your heavenly Father give the Holy Spirit to those who ask Him!

Notice the many scriptural images of God as Father. When we pray, for example, we are to think of the analogy of a father and child. This is the active love that God as Father expresses to His people. God as Father expressed His love for humanity in the active giving of His Son Jesus. Though God is the almighty creator, He is not the unmoved mover; He is God the Father who actively loves sinners and gives us access to Him in the person of His Son Jesus.

Study Questions
1. What is a "fundamental plank" in the theology of Nicea?
2. What is the focus of the Bible and history?
3. What is the "fullness of times" and where in the Bible is it found?
4. The gods of the classical world were really nothing more than what?
5. What is mythology and how does it differ from theology?
6. From where does our confession ultimately come?
7. How does a theological approach to knowing God affect other areas of knowledge?
8. How is the Christian confession different regarding the personal character of God? (And what difference does it make?)

9. Is access to the Father through Jesus optional?
10. What are some other Bible passages that relate to these issues?

5 Almighty Creator

The Almighty, Maker of heaven and earth . . .

> It is through the Father that all existence owes its origin. In Christ and through Christ He is the Source of all.[1]

One of the most basic ideas of Christianity is that God is the creator of all things. The fathers of the Council of Nicea said clearly that God is the almighty maker of heaven and earth, of all things visible and invisible. He has created not only everything we can see, but even the things we cannot see. This distinguishes God from His creation. Indeed, this creator/creature distinction is axiomatic to Christianity. In this sense, there may be nothing more fundamental for humans to comprehend than their status as creatures.

God is eternal and all other things are created; this is the simplest yet most profound reality that we must face. One noted father of our faith, St. Hilary, said it in the following way:

> He is infinite, for nothing contains him and he contains all things; he is eternally unconditioned by space, for he is illimitable; eternally anterior to time, for time is his creation. Let imagination range to what you may suppose is God's utmost limit, and you will find him present there; strain as you will there is always a further horizon towards which to strain. Infinity is his property, just as the power of making such effort is yours.[2]

---

1. St. Hilary, qtd. in Torrance, *Trinitarian Faith*, 77.
2. Ibid., 81.

Our status as creatures and God's status as creator are basic to Christianity. Indeed, much if not all that Christianity teaches flows like a fountain from the basic doctrine of creation. This is the fundamental starting point. Thus we discover that the creed is simultaneously descriptive and prescriptive. This means that if God is the creator and we are His creatures we owe him all that honor, obedience, and most importantly worship that is due to him as the Almighty creator.

The phrase of the creed "maker of heaven and earth" finds its origin in the Psalms. We should notice that it is in the context of redemption and salvation that we find the natural expression of praise to God as creator. The Psalmist says:

> Then the waters would have overwhelmed us, the stream would have gone over our soul; then the swollen waters would have gone over our soul. Blessed be the LORD, who has not given us as prey to their teeth. Our soul has escaped as a bird from the snare of the fowlers; the snare is broken, and we have escaped. Our help is in the name of the LORD, who made heaven and earth. (Ps. 124:4–8)

> I will lift up my eyes to the hills—from whence comes my help? My help comes from the LORD, who made heaven and earth. (Ps. 121:1–2)

Like the rest of the creed, this is not a bare theological proposition. The context won't allow us to imagine that this is the expression of some kind of an abstract ontological formula. To the contrary, this is the natural expression of praise and worship to the almighty creator God. Thus we say, "We praise you, O Lord, creator of heaven and earth."

God's work of redemption is linked here with His almighty work of creation. The sovereign God who made the heavens and the earth is also the God who saves sinners. If we anchor our minds back to the expression of God as Father, we are greatly helped. Remember, God is known first and foremost as Father because we know him through Jesus, His Son. Jesus is the means by which we understand the almighty creator God and the purpose connected to His work of creation.

The almighty power of God as creator is lovingly directed to men who need him. Thus His almighty power as creator provokes us to praise and worship. Indeed, praise is the only right and proper response of God's creatures. This is why the phrase "maker of heaven and earth" is so naturally linked with God's works of salvation.

It should strike us immediately that God would have never created man except as an expression of love. God as God didn't need to create us. In the eternal communion of the Trinity, God the Father, Son and Holy Spirit expressed love to each other and had no intrinsic need of creation. When He created the heavens and the earth, God wasn't lonely or bored. He did, however, chose to express His love to men in the act of creation. Creation was an expression of kindness and love towards humans. Consequently anyone who refuses to acknowledge this reality does not merely deny a theory of origins; this person participates in open rebellion to God.

The heavens and the earth did not exist eternally with God. Rather, God created all things by the word of His power out of nothing. All things have their origin in the creation of God, which provides a foundational way of thinking about the world and our place in it. This means that the Christian confession of God as almighty creator demands a worldview corresponding to it.

The men at the council did not reason solely from nature back to God. They would have considered this kind of reasoning as mythological and not theological. Rather, they began with God as the source of all things and then assigned creation its proper significance as God created and designed it. The Christian confession requires us to think of the world and our place in it always and only in relationship to God the creator. Torrance says rightly, "This in the last resort the inherent meaning and truth of the universe lie beyond its own limits in God who loves it, sustains it and undergirds it by his own divine reality."[3] Without the almighty creator there is nothing as we know it. What a pressing reality for the way we think and the way we live in this world!

Creation pushes us back to the helpful story of Adam and the naming of the animals. What was taking place in this story? Why did Adam name the animals? Was he pointing to the dove flying overhead and saying, "You are a dove"? Was he merely peering into the waters and saying, "You are a fish"? No, this story portrays Adam as assigning the creatures of the world their proper place in the divine scheme of things. Adam recognized that everything had a divine design. God created all things and Adam was to name them according to God's design. The whole theological character of naming things in the Bible involves the process of assigning something its divine significance. In this case, Adam had to name everything in accordance with God's purpose. Adam had no right as a creature to name the animals anything other than that which corresponded to their creation design. This is precisely why when he finished naming them he concluded that God had not yet created a suitable mate for him.

A similar "naming" continues to be the call of Christians today. We must assign all things in creation their divine purpose and place. Sin has caused men to rebel in this role, but the call remains the same. Indeed, if we attempt to redefine reality away from its creator's design, we pay a dear price for the confusion and chaos we create for ourselves.

This is exactly how Jesus Himself uses creation order when He teaches about marriage. This is how Paul uses creation design when he discusses the role of women in the church. Creation order and submission to the creator are intimately linked. They always have profound implications for moral and social order. If we reject the creator's design for us, we are like a man standing on a very tall building and denying gravity. He may deny as strenuously as he wants. The moment he jumps from the building, however, he will feel the truth of creation at work.

3. Torrance, *Trinitarian Faith*, 101.

The same is true for denials of creation order by legislators, educators, medical experts, scientists, fathers, and mothers.

Science, for instance, is one of many disciplines that must be done in submission to the reality of God as almighty creator. Far from hindering the progress of science, affirming creation enhances it. When a scientist assigns something its divine significance, he must do so by a thorough investigation of the thing itself. In this sense, he is at complete liberty to reason "from the bottom up." There is no dichotomy between science and Christianity.

It has become an assumption in modern and postmodern thinking that religion and science are separate; Christianity posits that they are one. If God is the almighty creator, then separating science from religious assumptions is as suicidal for science as for the man who jumps from the building denying gravity on the way down to his death. He is certainly free to deny and to jump, but the results are quite predictable.

Perhaps even more tragic is the moral and social chaos we create if we deny the doctrine of creation. What was once laughable and ridiculous is now being offered as a plausible even laudable alternative lifestyle. People exchange the truth for a lie and then call themselves "progressive."

The same kinds of things are asserted in the realm of legal theory. The doctrine of creation, however, has irresistible implications. For instance, is law really the result of a judge's decision or has the creator designed the world with moral purpose and meaning? The answer to these questions sets one on a course of life or death.

This is why evolution and Darwinism has had such a profoundly terrible effect on cultures who have believed it. If men are merely the result of random evolutionary forces then what is really wrong with exterminating the people who hinder progress? If you were a Jew in Nazi Germany or an unborn baby in most modern nations today the answer spells life or death. If men are made in the image of God per creation design, then we must respect human life and construct laws in accordance with divine design. Without this foundation, human life, and in particular the life of the weak and the helpless are at grave risk.

This also directs us away from a particularly pervasive obsession with individual rights and directs us back to the responsibility we have to the creator and from him to our neighbor. Certainly we don't deny the idea of God-given rights such as life and property. Still, the Christian is constantly directed towards the use of life and property to the glory of God and the welfare of his neighbor. Observing people today we would assume that the whole of life revolved around individual rights rather than divinely ordained personal responsibility. While we don't need to pit rights against responsibility, we do need to emphasize that rights cannot meaningfully exist without personal responsibility toward God our creator.

One basic link between creation and redemption is that of responsibility. If it is true that God created us, then we as His creatures owe him obedience and honor. Just as it is of the nature of God to be worshiped, it is also of the nature of men as creatures to worship him. Creation requires us to live in reference to God.

Connected to the whole issue of creation is the necessary doctrine of God's sustaining power of this creation:

> For by Him all things were created that are in heaven and that are on earth, visible and invisible, whether thrones or dominions or principalities or powers. All things were created through Him and for Him. And He is before all things, and in Him all things consist. (Col. 1:16–17)

Here we find that God not only created all things but He maintains them according to the same power by which He created them. Thus, we must live in ongoing submission to God's power to control His created order. God as the creator is also the one who sustains all things. His works of providence are His most holy wise and powerful, preserving and governing all His creatures and all their actions towards a good end. This is amazingly comforting in times of trouble. All of this of course not only has practical effects, but it has been commanded. Psalm 100 tells us to know that the Lord is God; it is He who made us and not we ourselves. This makes all the difference in the world.

The world is not eternal, but it is the result of God's continuing power to uphold all things by the word of His power. This has powerful implications for our worldview. Here as in so many portions of the creed, we are driven not so much to ponder as to worship: "I will lift up my eyes to the hills—from whence comes my help? My help comes from the LORD, who made heaven and earth" (Ps. 121:1).

STUDY QUESTIONS

1. What is one of the most basic teachings of Christianity?
2. How is the Creed both descriptive and prescriptive?
3. What is the origin of the phrase "maker of heaven and earth"?
4. Why is praise the only proper response to God as creator?
5. How is the creation an expression of divine love?
6. Why does a belief in creation carry moral consequences?
7. How is our worldview related to the creation?
8. What was Adam doing when he named the animals? How does this relate to our calling today? Give some examples of how cultures have strayed from this.
9. Which scriptures demand us to recognize God as creator?
10. Find some Bible passages not cited in the chapter that are relevant to these issues.

6   God of God

*We believe in one Lord, Jesus Christ, the only
Son of God, eternally begotten of the Father,
God from God, Light from Light . . .*

In this section of the creed, we have what may appear to be a
belabored and elongated approach to saying something rather
simple: Jesus Christ is fully divine and of the same essence as
God the Father. Why then does the creed outline a list of items
almost exhaustively arguing this point?

The catalyst of the Council of Nicea was Arianism. Quite
simply Arianism taught that Jesus Christ was not fully divine,
which strikes at the very heart of the gospel. After all, if Jesus
was not fully divine, then how could He accomplish the divine
work of salvation? If He was not fully divine, then He would
not have had the capacity to save men from the infinite wrath
of God against sin.

The first section of the creed had already established that
God the Father was eternal and divine. What about Jesus?
What is the relationship between God the Father and God the
Son? If in fact Jesus must be fully divine in order to accomplish
salvation, then the relationship between Jesus and God the Fa-
ther is critical. Indeed, Torrance states,

> the Patriarch of Alexandria soon realized and made it in-
> dubitably clear that the decisive issue for saving faith was
> the nature of the relation between Jesus Christ the incarnate
> Son and God the Father.[1]

The fathers were clear that the one God the Father almighty
was the same as the one Lord Jesus Christ. Hence, the creed

---

1. Torrance, *Trinitarian Faith*, 116.

addresses both the Father and the Son as the "one" and same God. They are referring to one and the same being. Yet the titles "Father" and "Son" do point to a distinction. This is the very distinction upon which Arius had capitalized. After all, Jesus is called "Son" and doesn't this imply something of a difference in His essence from His Father? Arianism focused on the phrase "only begotten," which is why the creed uses this phrase but also carefully qualifies it. How can Jesus who is called the "only begotten" be the same as the Father who is not "begotten"?

The phrase "only begotten" was a key phrase. It did, after all, originate in the Bible. Jesus is called the only begotten Son of God: "And the Word became flesh and dwelt among us, and we beheld His glory, the glory as of the only begotten of the Father, full of grace and truth" (Jn. 1:14).

Several other places in Scripture refer to Jesus as the "only begotten." What does this mean? The creed is clear that it doesn't mean "created." The phrase cannot mean an act of the will of God the Father.

If this were true, then Arius would be correct. Why couldn't he be correct? Again, the ultimate outcome of this question would not be determined by what has not been revealed, but by what has been revealed. And what has been revealed is that the only begotten Son of God is given to us "for us and for our salvation."

This kept men like Athanasius on an orthodox track in creating the creed. Athanasius was not distracted by the niggling philosophical questions that may have remained unanswered. He doggedly focused on the teachings of Scripture regarding the saving work of Jesus. If Jesus was sent to save sinners, then He had to be fully divine in order to accomplish this salvation. This fact would drive Athanasius in his writings and in his work on this issue. It became clear that understanding Jesus to be fully God meant that the decisive issue was His relationship to God the Father.

Consequently the orthodox fathers of Nicea did not allow a few phrases of Scripture to be taken out of the context of redemption. For instance, outside of the context of the redemptive work of Jesus, the phrase "only begotten" could possibly have indicated an act of the will. This is precisely what Arius had taught. Arius and his followers argued that Jesus had a temporal beginning because He was begotten. This hinges on understanding the phrase "begotten" as a temporal act of the divine will.

For Arius Jesus, the Son, was a created intermediary between the Father and His people. God the Father begot the Son in order to reveal Himself. This is so because the essence of the Father as "uncreated" is also inaccessible and unknowable. This is why Jesus was called the "only begotten." This is reasoning from a philosophical position about God back to the expression "only begotten." However, when this phrase was placed in the context of redemption, it pointed less to an act of the divine will and more to a relationship between the Father and the Son.

God used human language to reveal Himself to us, but human language has limitations. Standing alone or standing outside of the context of redemption, language is unsatisfactory. In a specific context, however, language is not only satisfactory but meaningful. The fathers' approach was very submissive to the reality that God in the Bible is using human language to communicate deep mysteries of faith. How does one interpret the language of the Bible? One must never attempt to take a single word or phrase out of the context in which it is used.

Here is where the orthodox fathers expressed a genuine humility to the words of Scripture without pressing them beyond what they actually say. The creed says what God says but it will not say more.

Athanasius exposes a fundamental weakness in Arian theology. The Arians had made a basic mistake in all of their philosophical discussions:

> Human procreation does in fact take place in time and in
> space. Human fathers are both older and separate from their

children. Begetting does involve division and separation. Not so, however, with God. The Arians have forgotten who the subject of the discussion actually is: The character of the parent determines the character of the offspring.[2]

This is a serious mistake in categories. The Arians were being mythological rather than theological. Mythology projects man's image or thoughts onto the divine. Theology is the opposite. Theology receives revelation from God and shapes ideas about God from this revelation. The Arians were attempting to project human categories onto God. This was illogical and inappropriate. The gods of the classical Greeks and Romans may have looked and acted like humans, but the God of the Bible is radically different.

Since God is eternal, His relationship with His Son is also eternal. Thus the Son is eternally begotten of His Father. This concept was so important that the phrases very God of very God and light of light were added. One could even say that Jesus is God of God truly. He is light of light because if you know the Son you know the Father. Jesus is "of" the Father in a unique way that all other things in creation are not. This is logical and corresponds properly to the revelation we have about God the Father and God the Son. Athanasius used the illustration of the relationship of the sun with the light it sheds.

> Just as the sun is inseparable from its rays (to be the sun is to shed light) so for the Father to be Father is to possess a Son. Whatever kind of begetting is involved in the relationship between Father and Son, this begetting cannot be external to their natural, inherent paternal and filial relationship.[3]

Athanasius and others who taught orthodoxy would not allow any phrases to be used without anchoring them in a redemptive context. Thus, every word about the Son had to be submitted to the redemptive context in which it was found

---

2. Christopher A. Hall, *Learning Theology with the Church Fathers* (InterVarsity, 2002), 40.

3. Ibid., 39.

as well as to the entire scope of the redemptive context of the whole Bible.

This was another reason the fathers understood the phrase "only begotten" not as expressing an act of the will, but as expressing an eternal relationship. Since the Bible speaks of the Son as fully God and since the Bible speaks of the Father as God, the phrase "only begotten" must be interpreted in this context. God the Father is eternal and as such He has eternally begotten the Son. This is what the church has called the eternal generation of the Son from the Father. There is never a time when the Father has not been the Father. This is why the creed is clear to say that the Son is begotten and that this cannot mean "created." He is begotten, not made.

The "only begotten" Son of God came to save sinners. The only begotten Son of God is also the Lamb of God who takes away the sin of the world.[4] He came to take for sinners what they could never do for themselves. He came to bear the infinite punishment of divine wrath. No mere human could bear such a penalty. The fathers anchored their interpretation of Jesus in connection to His work as redeemer. This means that Arius was not only wrong, but radically wrong. The damage such a view does to the work of salvation renders salvation impossible.

Since this was such a critical point the council employed the Nicene Creed's most pivotal word, *homoousios*, translated in English as "of the same essence." It may be one of the most famous words in the history of theology. Many creeds translate it as "one substance." However, since so many times we think of the word *substance* as physical stuff, the word *being* or *essence* works better. One may think that whatever the essence of that which constitutes deity actually is; it is the same for the Father and for the Son. They are essentially the same God, and so they chose to use the word *homoousios*. This word is so profound

---

4. See Colin Gunton, "And in One Lord, Jesus Christ . . Begotten, Not Made," in *Nicene Christianity: The Future for a New Ecumenism*, ed. Christopher R. Seitz (Grand Rapids: Brazos Press, 2001), 44.

because it is only a single Greek letter different than the other word the fathers had considered using.

There is a similar word, *homoiousios*, but the difference in meaning is worlds apart. That single letter changes the meaning to "of a similar essence." Rather than saying that the Son is of the identically same essence or being as the Father, this word says that the Father and Son are "similar." The council rejected this word, and a single Greek letter helped to clarify Christian doctrine for generations of orthodox believers throughout history.

So God the Father and God the Son are of the same essence or being. They are both equally God. Yet perhaps the brilliance of the word *homoousios* is that it also clearly establishes that the Father and the Son are distinct as persons. Hence, Athanasius said, "The Son is everything the Father is, except 'Father.'"[5]

Homoousios expresses a complete unity and oneness of essence while maintaining a distinction of persons. Torrance says,

> If the Son is eternally begotten of the Father within the being of the Godhead, then as well as expressing the oneness between the Son and the Father, *homoousios* expresses the distinction between them that obtains within that oneness. For nothing can be *homoousios* with itself, but one thing is *homoousios* with another.[6]

The fathers of Nicea argued for a unity of essence and diversity of persons. We can now comfortably use the phrase "one being, three persons." The Father, Son and Holy Spirit are all one God the same in essence and equal in power and glory. Yet, they are each distinct as persons. There is unity and diversity.

The same God who created the heavens and the earth is the selfsame God who re-creates man in salvation. Therefore, the creed says being of one substance with the Father, "by whom all things were made." This perfectly connects the Father and the Son as one and the same God. The same power that spoke

5. Athanasius, qtd. in Torrance, *Trinitarian Faith*, 124.
6. T. F. Torrance, *Trinitarian Faith*, 125.

all things into existence by the word of power is the very same power at work in us for our salvation.

The phrase "of one essence with the Father" is not only faithful to the Bible and theologically brilliant, but it offers a powerful evangelical call.

> It grounds the reality of our Lord's humanity, and of all that was revealed and done for our sakes by Jesus, in an indivisible union with the eternal being of God. It binds creation and redemption together in such a way that the creation is anchored in the love of God himself as its ultimate ground.[7]

The power of the gospel is brilliantly enhanced when we are able to say that God did not merely give some being similar to Himself. No, when God gave His only begotten Son on the cross for sinners, He gave Himself to us. We don't get a part of God in the giving of Jesus, we get God Himself. This illuminates something of the beauty of the biblical title *Emmanuel,* which means "God with us." We have a sure salvation because we have God with us. Here, as in all the parts, the creed calls us to wonder and worship in response to the gospel.

Study Questions

1. What did Arianism teach about Jesus' divinity?
2. Why did Jesus need to be fully divine?
3. What was a key phrase in this debate?
4. How did the context of "redemption" focus Athanasius and others in their work?
5. What was a fundamental weakness in Arian theology at this point?
6. How does God's eternal nature relate to the Son?
7. How did the fathers of Nicea "anchor" their teachings about Jesus in the context of redemption?
8. What does the word *homoousios* mean?
9. What does God give to sinners in the gospel?
10. Find some Bible passages not cited in the chapter that are relevant to these issues.

---

7. Ibid., 135.

7   For Us and for Our Salvation

For us and for our salvation He came down from heaven, was incarnate of the Holy Spirit and the Virgin Mary, and became truly human.

The love of God in salvation was the weight that anchored the fathers of Nicea from drifting into the dangerous waters of heresy. As they attempted to answer the flurry of questions that arose, they always kept one marker fixed; they never separated Jesus as the Son of God from Jesus as the Lamb of God who takes away the sins of the world. They would not allow philosophical or theological mysteries about who Jesus "was" to be detached from the revelation about what Jesus came "to do" as our savior. This acted as a virtual theological compass for the council of Nicea.

The words "for us and for our salvation," like so many words in the creed, don't merely suggest a bare theological truth; they offer the gospel. These are the sweet words of God's love that warm the hearts of those who hear them in faith. This is true philanthropy—literally, "love for men." This is a word that Athanasius used consistently and pointedly. While a host of philosophical and theological ideals were swirling around the halls of Nicea, ultimately God's "philanthropy" or love for men would drive the council to its final formulation.

Love is at the core of the incarnation; God so loved the world that He gave us His only Son, Jesus. Athanasius was central in developing this line of thought. He asked, "Why have you, being God, become man?"[1] Why did Jesus come down

---

1. Quoted in Torrance, *Trinitarian Faith*, 147. This would be the question that continued to drive the church to develop the doctrine of the atonement. In particular, St. Anselm's work *Cur Deus Homo* was the next major work in this vein.

from heaven to become a human being? The answer fills the pages of the Bible. God did this because He loves sinners. "For us and for our salvation" should resonate in our souls as we recite this great creed in worship.

The love of God for sinners accounts for God's humiliation as He came down from heaven. God obviously did not do all of this for His own sake. It is not as if He needed some earthly activity to divert him from cosmic boredom. No, it was not for His own sake but for our sake and for our salvation that God became man. Jesus had to become man because He was our covenant head or representative. Athanasius says,

> If Jesus Christ the incarnate Son is not true God from true God, then we are not saved, for it is only God who can save; but if Jesus Christ is not truly man, then salvation does not touch our human existence and condition.[2]

Yes, Jesus is the same substance or the same essence as God the Father. Having him as our covenant representative is at the heart of the gospel. Yet there are two sides of this theological equation. Not only did Jesus need to be fully God, but He also had to be fully human. "Everything," says Torrance, "would be emptied of evangelical and saving import if Jesus Christ were not fully, completely and entirely man, as well as God."[3] If Jesus were to take upon Himself the sins of the world, then He had to be divine. If He were to provide a just sacrifice in taking the place of humanity, He had to be a human being. He had to be both.

The perfect solution for His birth as a sinless human being came through the virgin birth. This portion of the creed hails almost directly from Matthew 1:20–21:

> But while he thought about these things, behold, an angel of the Lord appeared to him in a dream, saying, "Joseph, son of David, do not be afraid to take to you Mary your wife, for that which is conceived in her is of the Holy Spirit. And she

2. Athanasius quoted in *Trinitarian Faith*, 149.
3. Torrance, *Trinitarian Faith*, 146.

will bring forth a Son, and you shall call His name Jesus, for
He will save His people from their sins."

This birth account emphasizes the reality of Christ's humanity. He really was born a human being. Since Adam, the prior
federal head of humanity, was sinful, the Holy Spirit conceived
our Lord in the womb of the virgin. He was conceived of the
Holy Spirit to assure us He is God and from the Virgin Mary
to assure us He is man. As St. Augustine said, "From the father
he is the beginning of life, and from the mother he is the end
of death."[4]

God really, actually and historically became man for our
salvation. So the word of God says in John 1:1–14:

> In the beginning was the Word, and the Word was with
> God, and the Word was God. He was in the beginning with
> God. All things were made through Him, and without Him
> nothing was made that was made. . . . And the Word be-
> came flesh and dwelt among us, and we beheld His glory,
> the glory as of the only begotten of the Father, full of grace
> and truth.

This is quite clear. The same eternal Son who was with God
from the beginning and who was the very agent of creation is
the same God who became flesh. Jesus became a man. This
means that the eternal Son of God became a human being.
This is the incarnation. When this occurred Jesus did not become partially human. Jesus was not God covered in flesh. No,
He was truly and fully human. According to Athanasius, this
had to be the case if He were doing this on behalf of men.
Hence the phrase "for us and for our salvation."

There is always irony in the preaching of the gospel. Paul
says it is foolishness to those who are perishing. At the Nicene
Council the Arians thought they were making progress when
they searched for scriptures exposing the weakness, creatureli-
ness and mortality of Christ. His was a subordinate and ser-

---

4. Augustine quoted in Anthony M. Coniaris, *Orthodoxy: A Creed For Today*,
(Light and Life Publishing Company, Minneapolis, 1972), 116.

vant-like condition.[5] Hoping to exploit an apparent weakness in the nature and work of the Son, the Arians set this in contrast to the resplendent glory of the Father. Wasn't there an obvious contrast between the majestic glory of the Father and the servile condition of the Son? The answer was absolutely "yes."

Indeed, rather than rejecting the weakness and servility of the Son, Athanasius embraced it as fundamental to the whole work of salvation. Far from weakening the orthodox position, it actually enhanced the wonder of the incarnation. Athanasius used the irony of the incarnation not as a problem but as a point of praise. He says,

For it is a fact that the more unbelievers pour scorn on Him, so much the more does He make His Godhead evident. The things which they, as men, rule out as impossible, He plainly shows to be possible; that which they deride as unfitting, His goodness makes most fit; and things which these wiseacres laugh at as "human" He by His inherent might declares divine. Thus by what seems His utter poverty and weakness on the cross, He overturns the pomp and parade of idols, and quietly and hiddenly wins over the mockers and unbelievers to recognize Him as God.[6]

The creed provokes then not mere intellectual wonder, but worship and praise. The Christian today no less than the early church fathers should stand in awe at the incredible humility and love of God for sinners. Gregory of Nyssen exclaims,

Why did the divine being descend to such humiliation? Our faith staggers at the thought that God the infinite, inconceivable, and ineffable reality, who transcends all glory and majesty should be clothed with the defiled nature of man, so that his sublime activities are abased through being united with what is so degraded.[7]

---

5. Torrance, *Trinitarian Faith*, 154.
6. Athanasius, *De Incarnatione*.
7. Qtd. in Torrance, *Trinitarian Faith*, 153.

This calls something out in the soul of the Christian. What wonder and what praise belongs to this loving God! It is also a call for us to serve with the humility and love of God through Christ. This is precisely what Paul says in Philippians 2:3–7:

> Let nothing be done through selfish ambition or conceit, but in lowliness of mind let each esteem others better than himself. Let each of you look out not only for his own interests, but also for the interests of others. Let this mind be in you which was also in Christ Jesus, who, being in the form of God, did not consider it robbery to be equal with God, but made Himself of no reputation, taking the form of a bondservant, and coming in the likeness of men. And being found in appearance as a man, He humbled Himself and became obedient to the point of death, even the death of the cross.

Jesus was the servant as savior and continues to be the servant in heaven as our great high priest. Even now He actively intercedes for us. His incarnation as truly human teaches us the precious truth that our priest is able to sympathize with our weaknesses. He knows our frailties and He knows our experience as human beings struggling in a sin-scarred world. Christians don't pray to a priest who sits so far above and enthroned in heavenly splendor that He can't relate to us. No, we pray to someone who hears as a fellow traveler down the road of hardship and pain. Our Savior's death was for us and for our salvation. What a wonder! What a call to worship and praise!

For Jesus death was not the end, but only the beginning. Thus the humanity of Jesus emerges as central to His role as savior. Christ as the covenant representative became man so that He could take man's place. This was the great act of love to sinners—true philanthropy. The fathers at the council would not be lured into the speculation about the mysteries left unanswered. Divine love as revealed clearly in the Scriptures led them to confess only what was known. The unknown mysteries, though truly mysterious, did not detour them from speaking the clarity of God's love for sinners.

Study Questions

1. What acted as a theological compass for the fathers at Nicea?
2. What is at the core of the incarnation?
3. Why did Jesus need to be both God and man?
4. How did the Arians try to use the weakness of Christ to their advantage?
5. Did this work?
6. What did Athanasius think enhanced the wonder of the incarnation?
7. Why should we stand in awe of the incarnation?
8. How does the incarnation enable Jesus to sympathize with us?
9. Find some Bible passages not cited in the chapter that are relevant to these issues.

8 Crucified for Us

For our sake He was crucified under Pontius Pilate; He suffered death and was buried.

The whole idea of incarnation is absurd without the simultaneous idea of atonement. Why did Jesus need to do this? Why did Jesus need to come to earth in order to suffer and to die as a man? We already affirmed that it was for us and for our salvation. Without this loving purpose, the cross is not only absurd but absurdly brutal. Think of it—God the Father punishing the Son with suffering and death for something that was not necessary. No, the purpose of the incarnation is necessarily connected to the cross and the atonement. Jesus died in our place, punished for our sins. His death as our substitute makes atonement for us because He loves us and chose to save us.

This section is not as elaborate as the part dealing with Jesus' divine nature. One author notes, "The confession of Jesus' crucifixion passion and burial is notably terse and unadorned compared with the preceding sections that deal with His coessential deity and incarnation."[1]

The terse or plain character of this section probably lies in the lack of controversy surrounding it. Paul's confession in 1 Corinthians 15:3–4 is clear:

> For I delivered to you first of all that which I also received: that Christ died for our sins according to the Scriptures, and that He was buried, and that He rose again the third day according to the Scriptures . . .

1. David S. Yeago, "Crucified Also for Us under Pontius Pilate; Six Propositions on the Preaching of the Cross," *Nicene Christianity: The Future for a New Ecumenism,* ed. Christopher R. Seitz (Grand Rapids: Brazos Press, 2001).

Unlike some contemporary theologians, the fathers of Nicea did not suffer from doubts about the objective, historical reality of the crucifixion. Hence, they noted He suffered under Pontius Pilate as also outlined in the Bible. For this section the council simply quoted relevant portions of the Bible itself. There wasn't a need to elaborate or clarify since this was a long held reality of the faith.

Still, this section bears some amplification if only because so many people today who claim the name of Christianity also deny that the cross was for our sins as Paul stated. Some say the cross was merely an example of divine compassion and love. Jesus' death offers the supreme moral example for us to follow. This, however, misses the reality confessed in the creed that not only the whole of the incarnation, but the whole of human history hinges on this reality. The suffering, death and resurrection of Jesus was God's supernatural intervention that changed everything.

As we have already noted, God did not need to come to earth for His own benefit. He sent His only begotten Son because He loved sinners. St. Cyril says,

> We confess that he is the Son, begotten of God the Father, and Only-begotten God; and although according to his own nature he was not liable to suffering, yet he suffered for us in the flesh according to the Scriptures, and although impassible, yet in his crucified body he made his own the sufferings of his own flesh.

Jesus did not know suffering as God, but because of His great love for us He took on for us what was previously unknown and unnecessary for him. This is the downward movement of mercy that Paul describes for us in Ephesians 4:8–10:

> Therefore He says: "When He ascended on high, He led captivity captive, And gave gifts to men." (Now this, "He ascended"—what does it mean but that He also first descended into the lower parts of the earth? He who descended is

also the One who ascended far above all the heavens, that
He might fill all things.

Paul describes the condescension of Jesus who was enthroned in heaven and descended to earth for us. He not only
came to earth, but Paul describes a descent to death itself.

This is where the Nicene Fathers avoided the problems often
associated with the doctrine sometimes called the "harrowing
of hell." This is the idea that Jesus died and entered into Hell
itself. He remained there for three days and preached to the
doomed souls as described in I Peter 3:19. Then He broke out
of hell, bringing captives with him. This doctrine developed
throughout church history, but it does not find a place at Nicea. Indeed, the idea that Jesus preached to lost souls in hell did
not find it way into orthodox thinking at this point in church
history. In his day, St. Augustine even branded it heresy.[2]

The phrase "lower parts of the earth" does not make specific mention of the location of hell, but refers to the depth
of the descent of the incarnation. How low was Christ willing
to go on our behalf? He was willing to descend as low as man
can descend—that is, to death itself. This is exactly how Paul
describes it in Philippians 2. Death was the reference in Paul's
words and death is the focus of Nicea. We need to make sure
we see the phrase as a contrasting phrase to His former position in heaven. He was "far above all heavens," which speaks
of the range of our savior's condescension and then subsequent
exaltation.

Surely there was some measure of controversy over this doctrine, but the council clarified the words from the Apostle's
Creed which read, "He descended into hell." The council de-
cided that "He suffered and was buried" covered what needed
to be known. As in other parts of the creed, the fathers chose to
speak in the language of the Bible and allowed mysteries about
the mechanics of Jesus' death to remain a mystery.

---

2. See W. Hall Harris III, *The Descent of Christ: Ephesians 4:7–11 and Traditional Hebrew Imagery* (Grand Rapids: Baker, 1998).

The creed possesses a certain beauty in this regard. The fathers said what could be said and no more. Does this tell us everything there is to know about the death of our savior? No, but it tells us what is revealed about His death in the Bible and it tells us why we need to know it. It was for us and for our salvation.

Jesus suffering and death was a representative and substitutionary death on behalf of sinners. His death provided atonement for us. An earlier father, Irenaeus, had already begun to teach this idea. Irenaeus spoke of the incarnation and death of Jesus as a recapitulation on behalf of sinners. Jesus came to earth to recapitulate the different stages of man's life in order to take man's place in death. It falls short of course because Jesus did not recapitulate every possible stage of human existence. He was not for instance a husband or an old man. Still, we see the idea of Jesus living and dying as a substitute for sinners.

Through Jesus' obedient life and sacrifice sinners are made whole. As our representative Jesus reverses the penalty of sin and death for us. We were dead but in Christ we are made alive. Here also Athanasius expanded Irenaeus' work in his famous book, *De Incarnatione Verbi Dei*, or *Concerning the Incarnation of the Word of God*.

> Nor did He will merely to become embodied or merely to appear; had that been so, He could have revealed His divine majesty in some other and better way. No, He took our body, and not only so, but He took it directly from a spotless, stainless virgin, without the agency of a human father—a pure body, untainted by intercourse with man. He, the Mighty One, the Artificer of all, Himself prepared this body in the virgin as a temple for Himself, and took it for His very own, as the instrument through which He was known and in which He dwelt. Thus, taking a body like our own, because all our bodies were liable to the corruption of death, He surrendered His body to death instead of all, and offered it to the Father. This He did out of sheer love for us, so that in His death all might die, and the law of death

thereby be abolished because, having fulfilled in His body that for which it was appointed, it was thereafter voided of its power for men. This He did that He might turn again to incorruption men who had turned back to corruption, and make them alive through death by the appropriation of His body and by the grace of His resurrection. Thus He would make death to disappear from them as utterly as straw from fire.[3]

Jesus took for Himself the penalty due to sinners. In becoming human, Jesus became our substitute and took upon Himself the duty to pay our debt. He offered Himself in atoning sacrifice to God on our behalf. Torrance summarizes Athanasius' argument saying, "Christ has made our death and fate his own, thereby taking on Himself the penalty due to all in death, destroying the power of sin and its stronghold in death, and thus redeeming or rescuing us from its dominion."

The Hebrew word translated "atonement" means "a covering." In the work of Jesus, sinners have a covering for their sins. Theologians would continue to develop the whole concept of atonement. What for instance was this payment? St. Anselm would later liken it to the payment of debt to divine honor, which was offended by sin.

The idea of atonement as a forensic or legal payment for sin would also come to the fore. If sin was more than an insult to the divine honor, then it could also be understood as a payment of the penalty for sin, which was the satisfaction of divine wrath. If every sin deserves the infinite wrath and curse of God, then Jesus took upon Himself the infinite wrath of God. He became a curse for us so that we would not bear the curse. Indeed, we could never have borne such a curse. He is the second Adam who brings life instead of death. Paul describes this in Romans 5:12–21:

Therefore, just as through one man sin entered the world, and death through sin, and thus death spread to all men, because all sinned—(for until the law sin was in the world, but

3. St. Athanasius, *De Incarnatione*, VIII, 2.

sin is not imputed when there is no law. Nevertheless death reigned from Adam to Moses, even over those who had not sinned according to the likeness of the transgression of Adam, who is a type of Him who was to come. But the free gift is not like the offense. For if by the one man's offense many died, much more the grace of God and the gift by the grace of the one Man, Jesus Christ, abounded to many. And the gift is not like that which came through the one who sinned. For the judgment which came from one offense resulted in condemnation, but the free gift which came from many offenses resulted in justification. For if by the one man's offense death reigned through the one, much more those who receive abundance of grace and of the gift of righteousness will reign in life through the One, Jesus Christ.) Therefore, as through one man's offense judgment came to all men, resulting in condemnation, even so through one Man's righteous act the free gift came to all men, resulting in justification of life. For as by one man's disobedience many were made sinners, so also by one Man's obedience many will be made righteous. Moreover the law entered that the offense might abound. But where sin abounded, grace abounded much more, so that as sin reigned in death, even so grace might reign through righteousness to eternal life through Jesus Christ our Lord.

The substitutionary atonement of Jesus Christ makes the suffering and death of our savior both necessary and comprehensible. It is necessary if sinners are to be redeemed, and it is comprehensible because it makes sense of the suffering and death of the innocent Son of God. His suffering and death are meaningful and purposeful because they accomplished redemption for sinners. This, however, only explains our ability to understand Christ's death as a redemptive transaction. It does not, though, begin to plummet the depths of divine love that lay behind such a transaction.

Rather than explaining such love, it pushes us towards the inexplicable character of divine love. Why should God love us like this? He loves us in such a manner that He gave us His only begotten Son! What love is this? If we begin to comprehend this transaction aright, then we begin to be stunned at the depth of divine love for sinners.

What kind of love is so self-giving and sacrificial? What kind of love gives so extensively fully? Divine love exhausts the resources of the human mind to comprehend in this way. Indeed, the songs of the saints here on earth, and even in heaven, ring with wonder and praise for divine love.

Revelation 5:8–14 shows us this:

> Now when He had taken the scroll, the four living creatures and the twenty-four elders fell down before the Lamb, each having a harp, and golden bowls full of incense, which are the prayers of the saints. And they sang a new song, saying: "You are worthy to take the scroll, and to open its seals; for You were slain, and have redeemed us to God by Your blood out of every tribe and tongue and people and nation, and have made us kings and priests to our God; And we shall reign on the earth." Then I looked, and I heard the voice of many angels around the throne, the living creatures, and the elders; and the number of them was ten thousand times ten thousand, and thousands of thousands, saying with a loud voice: "Worthy is the Lamb who was slain to receive power and riches and wisdom, and strength and honor and glory and blessing!" And every creature which is in heaven and on the earth and under the earth, and such as are in the sea, and all that are in them, I heard saying: "Blessing and honor and glory and power be to Him who sits on the throne, and to the Lamb, forever and ever!" Then the four living creatures said, "Amen!" And the twenty-four elders fell down and worshiped Him who lives forever and ever.

STUDY QUESTIONS

1. Why is the creed's section on Christ's crucifixion notably short?
2. Why is there a need to elaborate today?
3. What is the doctrine of the "harrowing of hell?"
4. What did Jesus' death provide for sinners?

5. What is atonement?
6. According to Irenaeus, what was the purpose of the incarnation?
7. According to Athanasius what did Jesus' death do?
8. How did Anselm describe the atonement?
9. What does Romans 5 say about Christ's death?
10. What lay behind the atonement?
11. Find some Bible passages not cited in the chapter that are relevant to these issues.

9 The Resurrection

On the third day He rose again in accordance with the Scriptures . . .

Of all the doctrines by which Christianity stands of falls, this may be the most important. If there is no resurrection, there is no gospel. Hence, the creed makes the assertion that the resurrection is the hinge upon which the whole door of the incarnation either opens or closes. The resurrection, indeed, is the hinge upon which the whole of human history either opens towards a hopeful future or closes in gloom and death. This is certainly the way the Apostle Paul described the resurrection in his letter to the church at Corinth: "But if there is no resurrection of the dead, then Christ is not risen. And if Christ is not risen, then our preaching is empty and your faith is also empty" (1 Cor. 15:13–14).

Paul argues that Christianity is a mockery if there is no resurrection. He continues,

> And if Christ is not risen, your faith is futile; you are still in your sins! Then also those who have fallen asleep in Christ have perished. If in this life only we have hope in Christ, we are of all men the most pitiable. But now Christ is risen from the dead, and has become the firstfruits of those who have fallen asleep. For since by man came death, by Man also came the resurrection of the dead. For as in Adam all die, even so in Christ all shall be made alive. (1 Cor. 15:17–22)

We must conclude that churches that refuse to confess the resurrection have refused to confess the faith. This is no small matter. Carl E. Braaten notes,

The deepest divisions are no longer denominational, say, between Catholics and Protestants, Lutherans and Reformed, Evangelical and mainline churches, and so on. . . . The deepest fault line appears where faith and unbelief meet within the churches, among their theologians, bishops, and pastors. Nowhere is this more evident than in the matter of the resurrection of Jesus.[1]

Braaten rightly states that faith and unbelief are brought into sharp relief at the point of the resurrection. He writes in the same vein as Paul when he observes that "without the confession that God raised Jesus from the dead on the third day, Christianity has mutated into a different religion."[2]

Here he echoes the great Princeton theologian, J. Gresham Machen, who had already decried this reality in his famous 1923 book *Christianity and Liberalism*:

The present time is a time of conflict; the great redemptive religion, which has always been known as Christianity, is battling against a totally diverse type of religious belief, which is only the more destructive of the Christian faith because it makes use of traditional Christian terminology.[3]

The conflicts of which Machen wrote are the conflicts that arose as many scholars in the universities, seminaries, and churches began to question the historical reality of Jesus' resurrection. This sprang from what Machen called a kind of "naturalism" in which the supernatural elements that could not generally be explained in rational or scientific terms were dismissed as unreasonable and therefore incredible. This makes the human mind the crucible in which all doctrines of the faith were tested.

1. Carl E. Braaten, "The Reality of the Resurrection," *Nicene Christianity: The Future for a New Ecumenism*, ed. Christopher R. Seitz (Grand Rapids: Brazos Press, 2001), 107.

2. Ibid., 108.

3. J. Gresham Machen, *Christianity & Liberalism* (Grand Rapids: Eerdmans, 1990), 2.

The resurrection certainly qualifies as a supernatural event that science can not possibly duplicate. If the doctrine could not be submitted to the scrutiny of the human mind, then it must be incredible to the "wise." "Wise men" of all kinds emerged with more rational explanations for what must have happened to Jesus in life and, more importantly, at His death. As early as the eighteenth century, Reimarus went so far as to argue that the Christian religion was originally established by fraud on the part of Jesus' disciples. He theorized that they stole His body from the grave and waited long enough for the body to be unrecognizable. Then they fabricated the whole story of the resurrection and made it a basic part of the Christian religion.[4] Other more bizarre explanations for the resurrection were simply that Jesus had been prematurely buried then later revived in the coolness of the tomb. This is sometimes called the trance or swoon theory.

Critics of Christianity knew well that the resurrection was the key "myth" of the religion and that if one could undermine this doctrine, then so many of the other supernatural elements of the faith would dwindle away naturally. Consequently, they dismissed the resurrection and attacked it fiercely. This meant much more, however, than merely rejecting the resurrection. This meant rejecting the Jesus of the resurrection. This meant, as Paul has already noted, the rejection of the gospel itself.

Athanasius' insights on the centrality of theology over mythology apply not only to the classical "wise men" of his day, but to the modern "wise men" in our day as well. The resurrection, like so many doctrines of the faith, pushes rebellious people (especially modern and postmodern folks) to a breaking point of humility and submission. We can either resort to mythology, projecting our thoughts onto God, or we can submit to theology, receiving and resting in His word. This is very ironic, especially when you consider that modern theologians have dismissed the resurrection as "mythology."

4. Robert B. Strimple, *The Modern Search for the Real Jesus: An Introductory Survey of the Historical Roots of Gospels Criticism,* Presbyterian & Reformed, 1995), 18.

In fact, de-mythologizing the Scriptures became a hallmark of many "scholars'" work. Scholars in twentieth century began what Albert Schweitzer entitled his famous book: *The Quest of the Historical Jesus*. Later, Rudolf Bultmann and a whole host of other "wise men" sought to tear away the husks of ancient Christian mythology. Bultmann states, "An historical fact which involves a resurrection from the dead is utterly inconceivable."[5] The goal then was to peel back certain supernatural legends that encrusted the life of Jesus in order to discover the historical Jesus and thus the truth of the Bible.

The utter irony of this quest for the "historical Jesus" lies in its completely mythical character. Where, for instance, would one begin looking for the Jesus who was not raised from the dead? Herein lies the painful reality for modern and postmodern scholars; their Jesus is nothing more than a myth.

> This so-called historical quest is in actuality an attempt to desupernaturalize the only Jesus to whom we possess historical witness. . . . Clearly such a Jesus is not to be found anywhere in the entire biblical record. . . . It is the desupernaturalized Jesus which is the mythical Jesus, who never had any existence, the postulation of the existence of whom explains nothing and leaves the whole historical development hanging in the air.[6]

Hence Paul's criticism of the supposed "wise men" of his day is applicable to the "wise men" of our own day as well. Professing to be wise, they became fools in an ironic and self-defeating rebellion.

Self-defeating is certainly true. What is left to preach and to proclaim if there is no resurrection? This is a painful reality that many in churches today are being forced to answer. What is the church's mission if Jesus has not been raised from the dead? Again Braaten strikes the heart of the issue when he says,

---

5. Rudolf Bultmann, "The New Testament and Mythology," *Kerygma and Myth*, ed. H.W. Bartsch, trans. Reginald Fuller (London: SPCK, 1954), 39.
6. Strimple, *The Modern Search for the Real Jesus*, 9.

The most telling effect of the loss of resurrection faith in the mainline churches is the collapse of the world missionary movement. All the resurrection narratives are a summons to mission. . . . the missionary nature of the church from the beginning until now is grounded in the resurrection of the crucified Jesus.[7]

The testimony of the Scriptures as stated in the Nicene Creed is that on an actual day in history, which was three days after His crucifixion, Jesus rose from the dead. This is the actual historical Jesus in whom the church has always believed and in whom all the faithful must believe. The Nicene Creed clearly rejects the mythology and the legends of all other religions and replaces them with the historically objective work of God in the person of Jesus.

The Jesus of the resurrection is the God of the Bible and there is no separation. Braaten says correctly, "Faith in God is not separable from the belief that God raised the crucified Jesus from the dead."[8] Our hope is not a mythological hope, such as is found in other religions. These hopes fade with the death of their founders. Our hope is in the God who actually, historically, and objectively raised Jesus from the dead.

This is the heart of the good news of the gospel. Confessing, preaching and worshiping this God is the continuing mission of the church. God sent His only begotten Son to earth to take our place as sinners. This same Jesus triumphed over sin and death for us. What could possibly be better about the good news? This is the gospel that Paul preached when he stood at the Areopagus in Athens. This is the gospel that all the apostles preached as they went from town to town and from city to city spreading the good news of life in Christ. This is the gospel we also must preach today. In the resurrection resides the hope of all who are born to sin and death. The good news that Jesus was raised from the dead on the third day is the good news of life

---

7. Braaten, "The Reality of the Resurrection," 117.
8. Ibid., 110.

for the dead. Listen again to the Apostle Paul and be encouraged to worship your God!

> But now Christ is risen from the dead, and has become the firstfruits of those who have fallen asleep. For since by man came death, by Man also came the resurrection of the dead. For as in Adam all die, even so in Christ all shall be made alive. (1 Cor. 15:20–22)

Study Questions

1. Without the resurrection there is no what?
2. In what passage does Paul make this argument?
3. According to Braaten, what is the great fault line in churches today?
4. According to Braaten and Machen, what happens to Christianity without the resurrection?
5. What is naturalism?
6. What were some contrary explanations about the resurrection?
7. Modernists theologians dismissed the resurrection as a what?
8. Why are the quests for the "historical" Jesus so ironic?
9. According to Braaten, what collapses when churches reject the resurrection?
10. How is the Christian hope different from all other religions?
11. Find some Bible passages not cited in the chapter that are relevant to these issues.

10   The Ascension

He ascended into heaven and is seated at the right hand of the Father . . .

Like the incarnation, the ascension infuses history and our lives with the heavenly direction, eternal purpose, and meaning that we need so badly. We have a meaningful future because God rules it from heaven. The ascension of Jesus Christ not only requires us to look up to heaven but also requires us to look forward to what heaven will do here on earth. This is worth more than a little contemplation.

The ascension is extremely important to Christian theology. It provides the work of redemption with cosmic and historic consequences for the whole of human history. Salvation, then, is not merely something that happens to a collected group of individuals who get to escape hell. History bears the marks of the incarnation, and the future of the world is under the sovereign control of the ascended Lord. Even our calendar system marks the years appropriately with the Latin phrase *anno Domini* (A.D.), meaning "in the year of the Lord." Because of the ascension, history is moving forward to the coming judgment of all men. In the ascension we look up to heaven and thus we look forward to our future here on earth.

We may have a tendency to think of the ascension as an almost irrelevant doctrine. After all, isn't the ascension just the last part of the resurrection? Why is it significant that Jesus ascended into heaven and was seated there? The bodily ascension of Jesus doesn't seem to connect itself to anything very significant. Other doctrines may appear more important. For instance, the resurrection is immediately associated with victory over sin and death. This strikes us as more palatable and meaningful than the ascension.

The doctrine of the ascension of our Lord is oftentimes overlooked. Many other events in the life of Christ have found their way into popular Christian traditions. For instance, the birth of Christ is found in Christmas traditions, which may be the most popular. The resurrection of Christ is celebrated with Easter traditions all over the world. There is a constant harangue of books about the return of Jesus and His final judgment of the wicked. But what about the ascension? In some Protestant circles in particular, the ascension is virtually ignored.

The lack of attention presently given to the ascension of Jesus is revealing because you find that many churches spend a great deal of energy on bone-chilling end times stories. If some churches do not emphasize the rapture and end times fiction, they seem to have an almost obsessive interest in creating programs that attract people to their church. This does not include the ascension. The ascension draws our attention to Christ as the reigning king. Where would you go to find an emphasis on the rule and reign of Jesus as king?

Likewise, the ascension connects the church to the Great Commission and to the mission of the church on behalf of her king. The ascension of Christ into heaven indicates that the authority of heaven belongs to us here on the earth. This is almost exactly the way the Great Commission reads: "All authority has been given to me in heaven and on earth." Jesus then tells the church to make disciples. The ascension witnesses to the continuing work of Christ in heaven. Paul says exactly this in Ephesians 1:20–23:

> . . . which He worked in Christ when He raised Him from the dead and seated Him at His right hand in the heavenly places, far above all principality and power and might and dominion, and every name that is named, not only in this age but also in that which is to come. And He put all things under His feet, and gave Him to be head over all things to

the church, which is His body, the fullness of Him who fills all in all.

We are guilty of misunderstanding the words of our Lord upon the cross when He cried out, "It is finished" (Jn. 19:30). The Savior could truly say "It is finished" with regard to the work of redemption, which was accomplished on the cross. According to the usage of this expression, man's debt for sin could be marked "paid in full." But the Lord Jesus did not say "I am finished" in the sense that His work on earth was completed. Only His work of procuring men's salvation was finished. The work of proclaiming that salvation to men still continues. That is what Luke meant when he spoke of what our Lord "began to do and to teach" in the introduction to the book of Acts. The exciting thing to realize is that the ascension of our Lord was vital to the continuation of our Lord's work on earth through His body, the church.

The ascension was one of the principal events in New Testament redemptive history, marking the enthronement of the King of Kings and the Lord of Lords. From His humiliating birth among dirty animals, our Lord now ascends to His rightful place in the throne room of heaven. Still, there is even more. This event involves more than simply Jesus' return to heaven. Here He returns to heaven, having accomplished redemption. He is the triumphant redeemer-king. Hence, He is receiving power, glory, honor and His rightful place as ruler of His kingdom.

After divesting Himself of glory and taking on the form of a man; and having suffered all the temptations of man; and having been humiliated and subjected to pain and death at the hands of men; and having been abandoned by the Father and buried in death, our Lord Jesus Christ was exalted for it all. His exaltation should be celebrated as having a rightful place in the Christian view of the world.

We approach this New Testament story like we approach every other one: we look for its roots and origin in the Old

Testament. When we do this, we see that this often-overlooked event is the fulfillment of prophecies. The prophet Daniel, for example, says,

> I was watching in the night visions, and behold, One like the Son of Man, coming with the clouds of heaven! He came to the Ancient of Days, and they brought Him near before Him. Then to Him was given dominion and glory and a kingdom, that all peoples, nations, and languages should serve Him. His dominion is an everlasting dominion, Which shall not pass away, and His kingdom the one which shall not be destroyed. (7:13–14)

This is exactly what the apostles saw as the clouds of glory surrounded our savior. The cloud was not a "vaporous cloud" like the kind we see in the skies. Likewise, the cloud was not a puff of smoke. This was the glory-cloud presence of God, the cloud comprised of living creatures and angels.

Just as the angels announced His birth, so also in the ascension angels lifted up our Lord into heaven. The very throne room of God descends, in the cloud of creatures, to receive the third Person of the Triune Godhead, who immediately takes His rightful place. The angels flashing out from the glory-cloud lift Him up and bring Him to the Ancient of Days, just as Daniel had prophesied.

Daniel's prophecy is one of many prophecies of the coming king, who would be enthroned not as a normal king but as a priest-king after the order of Melchizedek. As the church launches out upon the Great Commission of the King of Kings, we do so with a heavenly/priestly mission. We do so under the leadership of our king who is like Melchizedek: both priest and king of the city of peace.

Psalm 110:1–6 is another prophetic example of Christ's kingship:

> The LORD said to my Lord, "Sit at My right hand, till I make Your enemies Your footstool." The LORD shall send the rod of Your strength out of Zion. Rule in the midst of Your

enemies! Your people shall be volunteers in the day of Your power; in the beauties of holiness, from the womb of the morning, You have the dew of Your youth. The LORD has sworn and will not relent, "You are a priest forever according to the order of Melchizedek." The Lord is at Your right hand; He shall execute kings in the day of His wrath. He shall judge among the nations, He shall fill the places with dead bodies, He shall execute the heads of many countries.

This prophecy of the enthronement of King Jesus exudes victory and power. Yet, this is clearly a victory and power that are dramatically unique. The rule of King Jesus is different. This king, unlike others who have come to rule upon the earth, rules through word and sacraments. Jesus has entered into the heavenly holy of holies and rules as our Great High Priest.

His rule finds its finest expression in the church of Jesus Christ. Indeed, the connections are not only obvious but also beautiful. We see this connection even as we look at the glory cloud coming back to earth at Pentecost. At Pentecost we see the glory of our ascended Christ brought back to earth in Acts 2. Heaven is brought to earth in great power and glory at Pentecost. The Holy Spirit is a gift from heaven as promised in Jesus' words from John.

In the church our priest-king Jesus rules from heaven. He rules upon the earth through the church in the word and the sacraments that He has given to her. The church sets about making disciples of the nations as she baptizes (sacraments) and teaches (word). There is no mistake that this commission is set in the context of the awarding of "all power in heaven and on earth."

In the ascension Jesus returns to His rightful place of power and glory as a conquering king. As such His Father gives Him the Kingdom as His reward for obedience. Christ does this all on behalf of His church. Paul makes this connection explicit in Ephesians 4:7–13:

But to each one of us grace was given according to the measure of Christ's gift. Therefore He says: "When He ascended on high, He led captivity captive, and gave gifts to men." (Now this, "He ascended"—what does it mean but that He also first descended into the lower parts of the earth? He who descended is also the One who ascended far above all the heavens, that He might fill all things.) And He Himself gave some to be apostles, some prophets, some evangelists, and some pastors and teachers, for the equipping of the saints for the work of ministry, for the edifying of the body of Christ, till we all come to the unity of the faith and of the knowledge of the Son of God, to a perfect man, to the measure of the stature of the fullness of Christ.

There is no mistaking Paul's connection with the victorious ascension of King David to the city of Jerusalem and the ascension of Jesus to heaven to rule His new Jerusalem the church. At Pentecost God sent His Spirit from heaven in a cloud of glory. He gave ministers to the church who ruled with word and sacrament in the power of the Holy Spirit.

In this passage from Ephesians, Paul uses Psalm 68:18 as an illustration of how Christ accomplished redemption for us and now bestows us with gifts from heaven. Psalm 68 was a victory hymn composed by David to celebrate his conquest of the Jebusite city of Jerusalem and the triumphant scene of God's ascent up Mt. Zion to the throne of Jerusalem.

There is a resurrection reversal in the Psalm as Paul uses it. In the original, the Psalmist says, "You received gifts from men, even your enemies." Here Paul has Jesus not receiving gifts, but giving them, as recorded in Samuel. The basic wording comes from Psalm 68, but it is not a direct quote. Hence, it appears that Paul combined the Psalmist's account with the actual account from Samuel and applies it to Jesus.

After King David defeated the enemies of God in the famous city of Jerusalem, he brought the spoils of war to his people along with the Ark of the Covenant and celebrated before the Lord. It was in the midst of this glorious celebration that he and the people sang and danced and ate and drank. Here David's heart was filled with generosity to his people showering them with gifts amidst his celebration of victory. Most importantly God had triumphed on Mt. Zion because the ark was finally in its appointed place. Listen to Samuel's account in 2 Samuel 6:12–19:

> So David went and brought up the ark of God from the house of Obed-Edom to the City of David with gladness. And so it was, when those bearing the ark of the LORD had gone six paces, that he sacrificed oxen and fatted sheep. Then David danced before the LORD with all his might; and David was wearing a linen ephod. So David and all the house of Israel brought up the ark of the LORD with shouting and with the sound of the trumpet. So they brought the ark of the LORD, and set it in its place in the midst of the tabernacle that David had erected for it. Then David offered burnt offerings and peace offerings before the LORD. And when David had finished offering burnt offerings and peace offerings, he blessed the people in the name of the LORD of hosts. Then he distributed among all the people, among the whole multitude of Israel, both the women and the men, to everyone a loaf of bread, a piece of meat, and a cake of raisins. So all the people departed, everyone to his house.

This is just as the prophets of the Old and New Testaments had predicted. In Luke 1:32–33 we read this: "He will be great, and will be called the Son of the Highest; and the Lord God will give Him the throne of His father David. And He will reign over the house of Jacob forever, and of His kingdom there will be no end." We see here that David is a type of Christ. He ascends victoriously to his throne on the mountain and gives gifts to his servants. Paul tells us that Jesus conquered death even as David had conquered the Jebusites. As enemies of God, the Jebusites had held the holy city captive, but now they were captives of the king. The text reads literally that he captured—or conquered—captivity.

In the resurrection, Jesus, as a king greater than David, conquered the last stronghold against the people of God: death. In the ascension, He ascends into heaven as David had ascended to his throne and makes a public display of his enemies. He is now in "session" or seated as the ruling king. He rules and will continue to rule until the final judgment. Because of the ascension we know for certain that we all live life under the scrutiny of heavenly judgment, and all men will one day give an answer for what they have done. What a sobering thought!

Because the ascension is about the enthronement of Christ the king, it demands a certain earthly/heavenly-mindedness in submission to His rule. Have you ever heard someone say, "they are so heavenly minded that they are of no earthly good?" If you have heard this, then you know that they are not talking about someone who practices true heavenly thinking. The Bible demands us to be heavenly-minded, which translates into earthly activity. If you are truly heavenly-minded, then you will be active here on earth.

We are not on the horns of a dilemma. We do not need to be either heavenly-minded or earthly-minded. Rather, we are to be heavenly-minded so that we can be of some earthly good. You will notice that especially in Pauline theology we see that our heavenly existence in Christ is always connected with the required activity we have here on the earth. Consider Colossians 3:1:

> If then you were raised with Christ, seek those things which are above, where Christ is, sitting at the right hand of God. Set your mind on things above, not on things on the earth. For you died, and your life is hidden with Christ in God. When Christ who is our life appears, then you also will appear with Him in glory. Therefore put to death your members which are on the earth: fornication, uncleanness, passion, evil desire, and covetousness, which is idolatry. Because of these things the wrath of God is coming upon the sons of disobedience, in which you yourselves once walked when you lived in them. But now you yourselves are to put off all

these: anger, wrath, malice, blasphemy, filthy language out of your mouth. Do not lie to one another, since you have put off the old man with his deeds, and have put on the new man who is renewed in knowledge according to the image of Him who created him. Therefore, as the elect of God, holy and beloved, put on tender mercies, kindness, humility, meekness, longsuffering; bearing with one another, and forgiving one another, if anyone has a complaint against another; even as Christ forgave you, so you also must do. But above all these things put on love, which is the bond of perfection. And let the peace of God rule in your hearts, to which also you were called in one body; and be thankful.

It may seem obvious to many of us, but it is a real problem for others. In fact, it does provide a real tension. Our citizenship is with Christ in heaven. This, however, requires active citizenship here on earth in whatever country He has providentially placed us in.

We see the beautiful heavenly vision of earthly saints in the lives of some of the Puritans. Leland Ryken's book *Worldly Saints* captures so aptly the story of Puritan history. The Puritans believed that they were pilgrims on the earth, but pilgrims with a heavenly mission. They believed that the temporary suffering they endured on the earth had a heavenly destiny. Consequently, they suffered hardships, fought wars and gave their lives in the cause of Christ. We may not agree with everything they taught or pursued, but their sense of heavenly destiny is worthy of anyone's admiration.

Because the Puritans believed that Jesus was their heavenly king, their lives here on earth were different. Heavenly-mindedness translates into a genuine concern for politics, education, business, and anything else that touches our lives here on the earth. Because they lived their lives in reference to the ascended Lord of glory, they made a difference here on the earth. They really did believe the part of the Lord's prayer which petitions the Lord to bring His kingdom to earth just as it is in heaven.

The ascension gives us a heavenly perspective for life here on earth.

Indeed, one could argue that the doctrine of the ascension is closely connected to every major political/cultural development that has driven earthly powers to respect the laws of heaven here on earth. The whole concept of constitutional restraints on rulers has intimate connection to the doctrine of the ascension. Because of the rule of Jesus, there is no authority here on earth that doesn't have reference to the ultimate rule of the exalted king. Because of the ascension no authority here on earth may rightly claim absolute authority. All earthly authority is limited to and has reference to the heavenly authority of Jesus. All earthly authority is delegated and limited to the direction of the ascended Lord of glory. Because of the ascension all earthly authority finds its meaning, direction and purpose in the ascended Lord Jesus. Families, churches and civil governments all derive their meaning and purpose from the ascension of Jesus. To say that the ascension has had profound implications for modern social/political developments is a vast understatement.

Another corollary of Christ's powerful enthronement in the ascension is that it cures us of self-centeredness. The world revolves around Christ as king; not us. In fact, the apostles had to be reminded of this at the instant the ascension was finished. They were told to stop gazing up and to start moving forward.

We are often like the apostles, tending to think that we are at the center of everything. We laugh sometimes at the obvious nature of children to think primarily of themselves. If your children are like mine at Christmas, you probably have to remind them to be thankful for what they get. On one occasion, we got a trip to California and no other gifts. This is hard for a child to accept when others are opening actual packages. Even sometimes when a child opens a present he didn't exactly hope to get, he shows his lack of thanks by making the obvious face that every parent is embarrassed to see—squinting eyes and furrowed eyebrows that say, "That wasn't what I wanted!" They think that whatever happens, happens with respect to them. Teenagers often exhibit this same attitude in extreme measures: they can't walk into a room without thinking that everyone is staring at them.

We even sometimes treat the ascension of Christ in this same way. "If there is a 'coming,' then the 'coming' must be to us! Likewise, if there is 'departure,' then the departure is from us!" We see everything is in relation to *us*. This is the thinking of egocentric, fallen man. But everything is not for us; everything is not centered around us; and comings and departures are not, necessarily, to us and from us. The ascension teaches us that everything is centered on and revolves around Jesus Christ. If we look up humbly to the King of Kings, then He will lovingly direct our eyes forward to a life filled with heavenly meaning and eternal purpose. Praise God for the ascension of Jesus!

The ascension always inspires heavenly hope in the hearts of the faithful. We are called upward and forward in the ascension. We are called in the same way the church was first called by it:

> So then, after the Lord had spoken to them, He was received up into heaven, and sat down at the right hand of God. And they went out and preached everywhere, the Lord working with them and confirming the word through the accompanying signs. Amen. (Mk. 16:19–20)

Study Questions
1. How does the ascension infuse history with meaning?
2. What does the Latin phrase *anno Domini* mean?
3. How does the ascension connect the church to the Great Commission?
4. How are the ascension and Christ's enthronement connected?
5. What Old Testament prophecy speaks of the ascension?
6. How is the ascension connected to Melchizedek?
7. What Psalm refers to this event?
8. How is the ascension connected to the church's rule on earth?
9. How does Psalm 68 relate to the ascension?

10. What do we mean by saying "Jesus is the greater David?"
11. How does the ascension require us to be "worldly saints?"
12. How does the ascension fight self-centeredness?
13. Find some Bible passages not cited in the chapter that are relevant to these issues.

11 Ascended and Coming Again

He will come again in glory to judge the living and the dead, and His kingdom will have no end.

Because of the doctrine of the ascension, Christianity requires a distinct philosophy of history. Indeed, the ascension as described in Psalm 110 connects history to a destined end or purpose. The psalmist says, "The LORD said to my Lord, 'Sit at My right hand, Till I make Your enemies Your footstool'" (vv. 1–2).

The rule of Jesus is directed towards an ultimate judgment and consummation. History is not a meaningless series of disconnected events; to the contrary, history contains specific objectives related to the personal rule of Jesus Christ. Jesus did not merely float up in a rain cloud away from the earth in the ascension. He was enthroned in heaven to rule and to direct the unfolding events of history. Remember, that He was surrounded with the glory cloud presence of God and ascended to His rightful place as the redeemer-king. There He rules over all things unto the blessing of His church and towards a very specific purpose.

History has meaning and a coherent direction because of this reality. History is not just meandering along an unknown path towards an unknown future. Christ will rule, says the psalmist, until all His enemies are made a footstool. This is the determined end, which is the judgment of all men. History then moves along the destined path set for it by the sovereign king of glory who has ascended to His throne in heaven.

This philosophy of history was most notably developed in the classic work of St. Augustine entitled *The City of God*. The

Christian philosophy of history is radically different from so many of the popular classical views of history prevalent at the time of the writing of the Nicene Creed. Some of the pagan historians in the days of the creed wrote history as if it were a meaningless cycle of events. History was described as moving in cycles of growth and cycles of decline. This is sometimes described with the metaphorical images of precious metals. They saw history as a series of golden ages followed by the inevitable declining ages of silver, bronze, and iron. This cyclical view of history was common to classical, pagan thinking.

St. Augustine, a church father from North Africa, wrote about history as a Christian who confessed the Nicene Creed. History was not a meaningless cycle of events, but rather was moving towards a meaningful conclusion. Augustine lived and wrote in a period of history in which thousands of people were shocked and shaken at the fall of Rome. When Rome fell in A.D. 476, the unthinkable had occurred. It was unthinkable because Rome had been called *urbs aeterna*, the eternal city. Augustine wrote *The City of God* in response to the fall of Rome, the eternal city, to marauding barbarians.

How could it be that the eternal city of Rome had fallen? This lament sounds similar to that of the prophet Habbakuk, who could not believe that God would judge the nation of Israel, especially using an evil nation. The ancient Israelites thought of Assyria like the Romans thought of the barbarians—as the embodiment of vulgarity and evil. How could evil be triumphing over good?

Since so many men and women in the ancient world had placed their whole hope of the future in the Roman Empire, they were devastated when Rome fell. Because the nation in which they had placed their trust had been defeated, they became unhinged. This is a familiar story. If your life depends on the success or failure of nations and kingdom of the earth, then your life will unravel as those nations face failure or decline. What a terrible way to live!

Augustine recognized the chaos of such a view. He offered the ancient world a meaningful and hopeful alternative. Kingdoms of the earth come and go, but the kingdom of God stands forever. This became the underlying theme of his aptly titled book: it is the City of God which is the focus of history. History is the unfolding of God's sovereign plan that brings all things to a foreordained conclusion on behalf of His kingdom.

The phrase "He shall judge the living and the dead" instills purpose in our personal lives in the overall scheme of history. Not only is history moving towards an ultimate judgment, but every man in history will face a time at which all his actions will be judged. This gives history and our role in it a very personal perspective as a Christian. For instance, no matter what kind of an apparent injustice or inequity occurs in time and in history, Christians can remain patiently faithful because we serve the God who will one day bring all things to justice. No man will escape the judgment of God forever.

We must hold this truth close to our hearts in times of apparent injustice here in time and history. One does not need to live very long to notice that rewards and punishments don't always correspond justly. We could all name a person, or perhaps even entire groups of people, who have apparently escaped a just judgment against them. In fact, many of us are personally forced to reckon with this on a daily basis.

This reality can frustrate people to draw poor conclusions. Because we see inequity and injustice, do we determine that there is therefore no judge on the earth? Some conclude that there may be a judge, but He must not be just. Christians have a perfectly reasonable but practically painful answer. We acknowledge that there is a judge, and while He does not always provide immediate judgment here on earth, He will most certainly provide ultimate judgment to all men.

The arrogant will not temper their pride to this reality. They will demand immediate justice and will not wait upon the Lord. Waiting for such judgment teaches us tremendous patience as well as dependence on God in deep ways. This is precisely what restrains the faithful Christian from seeking personal vengeance. Vengeance belongs to the Lord and we wait on him patiently. We are people who live with an eternal perspective. This enables us to live with a certainty and purpose that befits a people of destiny in spite of events we feel are the very crumbling of history around us.

No matter what happens historically to this or that nation, the Christian lives with regard to the ascension and the rule of heaven. The future belongs to Jesus and the believer lives with regard to the certainty of the future judgment of all men. This drives the Christian to live as Christ lived: with humility.

The king who has risen from the dead in conquest is also the one who will judge all men. Judgment is certain and this part of the creed acts as a serious warning to all of us. Rest assured that as certainly as Christ rose from the dead and ascended into heaven, He will come again to judge all peoples. Pearson says,

> If we do but reflect upon the frame and temper of our own spirits, we cannot but collect and conclude from thence that we are to give an account of our actions, and that a judgment hereafter is to pass upon us. There is in the soul of every man a conscience and whosoever it is, it giveth testimony to this truth.[1]

A very sobering and oftentimes embarrassing experience is for us to have someone discover our actions that we intended to remain secret. This is especially shameful if those actions were deliberately sinful and we intended for them to remain secret. We yell in anger, for example, at our children, only to discover that an unexpected guest has been waiting for us at our front door, and has heard every word. When we find out that they heard our outburst we are embarrassed and humiliated. If this is a sobering thought, how much more should we be shaken to the core to know that all of our actions come under the scrutiny of Almighty God?

---

1. John Pearson, *An Exposition of the Creed* (London: George Bell and Sons, 1876), 448.

Divine judgment, then, becomes a powerful part of the gospel message. The good news cannot be understood without the corresponding bad news. This was certainly part of the apostolic message. In Acts 24:25 we find Paul reasoning with Felix about many things, including the coming judgment of all men. Neither kings nor governors are exempt from this judgment. Paul reasons in the same way when he preaches to the philosophers of Athens in Acts 17:31. An even more powerful statement comes from Paul in Romans 2:5–8:

> But in accordance with your hardness and your impenitent heart you are treasuring up for yourself wrath in the day of wrath and revelation of the righteous judgment of God, who "will render to each one according to his deeds": eternal life to those who by patient continuance in doing good seek for glory, honor, and immortality; but to those who are self-seeking and do not obey the truth, but obey unrighteousness—indignation and wrath. . . .

Clearly the creed reflects the word of God in calling all men's attention to the coming judgment of God. We must also call all men everywhere to the judge of all the earth, Jesus.

Yes, it is Jesus who personally judges all men. Jesus is the one to whom all judgment has been entrusted, because His work of redemption in time and history gives him the right to judge. He has accomplished redemption and demands all men to repent and turn to him one way or the other. This future is certain because of His redemptive work.

> And being found in appearance as a man, He humbled Himself and became obedient to the point of death, even the death of the cross. Therefore God also has highly exalted Him and given Him the name which is above every name, that at the name of Jesus every knee should bow, of those in heaven, and of those on earth, and of those under the earth, and that every tongue should confess that Jesus Christ is Lord, to the glory of God the Father. (Phil. 2:8–11)

This whole scene is most definitely connected to the ascension, and the creed has it properly connected as well. The accomplished work of redemption in history demands a redemptive view of the future. Jesus has accomplished redemption and just as certainly as He has accomplished it, He will bring all things to their proper conclusion.

This drives us to godly living and the hope of glory, as well as to continual humility toward Jesus. All men will bow down to Jesus one way or another. The Christian hopes in the future because he knows that for those who humbly submit to him their judgment has been taken from them and satisfied in Christ's work on the cross. We will face the judgment, but our sentence will be different than those outside of Christ, being judged under grace rather than the law.

This gives us hope for the future and strength to live today in faithfulness. Our future does not depend on any nation or kingdom on earth. Our future is as steady as an eternal city because it is the city of God. Thus the creed agrees with Scripture, stating, "whose kingdom shall have no end."

History will have a conclusion, which will be the judgment of all men. This will not, however, end the rule and reign of Christ in heaven. He will rule forever. Indeed, Daniel says this about it:

> I was watching in the night visions, and behold, One like the Son of Man, coming with the clouds of heaven! He came to the Ancient of Days, and they brought Him near before Him. Then to Him was given dominion and glory and a kingdom, that all peoples, nations, and languages should serve Him. His dominion is an everlasting dominion, which shall not pass away, and His kingdom the one which shall not be destroyed. (Dan. 7:13–14)

STUDY QUESTIONS

1. The doctrine of the ascension requires what?

2. Explain why the ascension gives history meaning.
3. What was the title of St. Augustine's famous book on history?
4. What did pagan historians believe about history?
5. What event shocked the classical world and why?
6. According to Augustine, what is the focus of history?
7. What does the creed say makes history personal?
8. How does this offer practical/personal help in our lives?
9. How is it sobering to live with this doctrine?
10. How does divine judgment play a role in the gospel?
11. How does it provide hope and incentive to faithfulness?
12. Find some Bible passages not cited in the chapter that are relevant to these issues.

12

The Holy Spirit

We believe in the Holy Spirit, the Lord, the giver of life . . .

Like all the doctrines of this precious creed, the Christian believes in the Holy Spirit not merely as an intellectual matter, but as a matter of life and death. We believe in the Holy Spirit, the Lord and giver of life. This truth lends itself to liturgy and worship. When we worship our God, we not only confess with our mouths the reality of the Holy Spirit as God, but we cling to the Holy Spirit as our life and hope. Confessing this truth, we bask in the gentle and even fragrant life that comes to us through the Holy Spirit.

The Holy Spirit brings beauty and order to that which is formless and void. Such is the image of the creation account and such is the comforting paradigm of redemption for all who follow in the way. The Spirit is light and life to the true believer. In the creation story, God created all things and made them at first formless and void. It is the Spirit of God hovering over the darkness which provides us the portrait of light bringing hope to the darkness. The Spirit of God also breathes life into the motionless body of our first father Adam. Hence, light and life are perfect images for the blessed Holy Spirit. These are images that provoke warmth and comfort in the heart of the Christian.

The Holy Spirit is particularly connected to our comfort and hope. This is so because in the Spirit of God we have God Himself coming to us and redeeming us. This is after all the heart of the covenant promise of Emmanuel, "God with us." Christians must believe this. Without Jesus we would have no hope; so without the Spirit we would not have Jesus. The Nicene Creed outlines a belief in the Holy Spirit as a necessary element of true life and of the true faith.

At the meeting of the Council of Nicea in 325, expressing belief in the Holy Spirit was not especially controversial. Indeed, the council spoke of the Holy Spirit only in the last single sentence, saying simply, "We believe in the Holy Spirit." The more developed phrase we use today was added at the Council of Constantinople in 381. From Nicea to Constantinople the doctrine of Holy Spirit, like the doctrine of Christ, came under serious and relentless attack. Many who had denied the divinity of Jesus also attempted to deny the divinity of the Holy Spirit.

The church responded properly to this threat. The Holy Spirit is the only means by which the life-giving redemption of the Son of God is applied to men. God comes to men through the Spirit enlightening their minds in the knowledge of Christ. The Spirit both persuades and enables men to embrace Jesus Christ as He is freely offered to them in the gospel. The life-giving character of the Holy Spirit was of course not original to the men of Nicea. To the contrary, in Genesis the Spirit of God breathed the breath of life into Adam. What an image!

The breath of God in the person of the Spirit is not an impersonal force, power, or emission of God. This was a key issue in the ancient world. We can easily recognize the creed's timely help not only for our ancient fathers, but likewise for us today. Eastern forms of religion, for instance, often speak of their gods as an impersonal force. The wildly successful Star Wars movies of the late twentieth century have popularized the notion that divine forces live and move in all of us all the time. This is not a Christian belief. The Holy Spirit is not the "force" or the "spirit" of some world-soul. He does not animate all things in this sense.

We are guarded from this idea because the Bible reveals to us that the Holy Spirit is God Himself. The Holy Spirit cannot be detached from the essence of God the Father or God the

Son because the Holy Spirit is God. This is why, as Torrance states, "the Holy Spirit was inseparably associated with the Father and the Son in praise and worship." Here again we do not discover something in the life of the church that differs from the Scriptures themselves. The Bible teaches the Trinity. The Gospel of Matthew gives us the formula for baptism "in the name of the Father, Son, and the Holy Spirit." All those who enter the church do so confessing this truth.

The baptismal formula is Trinitarian and requires submission to the Holy Spirit. This is why the Nicene Creed properly affirms the truth of the Spirit of God as the "Lord." This is the divine name for God also ascribed to Jesus. The Holy Spirit no less than Jesus is our master. Yet, the role of the Holy Spirit can sometimes cause us to forget this truth.

The Holy Spirit's role in our lives is not the same as that of the Father or the Son. While He is equally divine His role is unique. There is unity and diversity in how God masterfully redeems His people from their sins. There is then an equality of essence with a distinction in function, and the Holy Spirit functions in a very self-diminishing manner.

For instance, the Holy Spirit of God does not draw attention to Himself in salvation; rather He points us to the Father and the Son. The Holy Spirit does not bring to us any independent knowledge of God nor even independent knowledge of Himself per se; instead, He reveals to us the Father and the Son. Athanasius says, "He comes to us as the Spirit of the Father and of the Son, revealing the Father in the Son and the Son in the Father, and thus as himself God through whom God reveals himself."[1]

One man likens the Holy Spirit to a light that shines on a beautiful cathedral. The light is constantly illuminating the stones, sculptures and designs. We see the light, but only as a means of illuminating the cathedral. The Holy Spirit reveals Himself to us as He enlightens us in the knowledge of Christ.

---

1. Quoted in Torrance, *Trinitarian Faith*, 203.

The Spirit of God makes known to us what otherwise could not be known of God.

The Holy Spirit also gives us life. He does what theologians call a work of regeneration. The Apostle Paul describes us being "dead" in transgressions and sins, but then by the work of the Holy Spirit we are made alive in Christ. How does this happen? It happens as the Holy Spirit gives life to spiritually dead sinners.

The Holy Spirit gives us light and life. He personally reveals to us the grace of God. Again, we should notice that this work is not impersonal, but personal. The Holy Spirit is a person and personal. As we mentioned already, the Holy Spirit is not a "force."

The Bible refers to him with the personal pronoun "He," not "It." He is said to be like the wind in His effects, but He is not the actual wind. He is a person. He is called our "comforter" in John 14:16. The Holy Spirit has intellect, for He is said to know the things of God. He also has feelings, as noted in Romans 8:27. Paul appeals to us on the basis of the love of the Holy Spirit in Romans 15:30: "Now I beg you, brethren, through the Lord Jesus Christ, and through the love of the Spirit, that you strive together with me in prayers to God for me. . . ."

The Holy Spirit is a person who loves us. He regenerates us, teaches us, guides us, works in us, searches our hearts, speaks to us, testifies to us of the love of God, convicts us of our sins, and intercedes on our behalf. He plays multiple roles in our lives and serves us lovingly and always personally. He is our ultimate friend. As such, the Holy Spirit dwells in a believer's heart. Is it possible from this massive biblical witness to think of the Holy Spirit as anything other than personal?

If we think of the Holy Spirit as something other than a personal being, we will tend to disregard him and grieve him. Indeed, defining someone as less than a true person has led to great mistreatment throughout human history. The Nazis regarded the Jews as less than true persons, and look what they justified. Some slave owners defined their slaves as less than personal and used this to perpetrate various abuses against them. Abortionists redefine unborn babies as something other than personal beings, and as such they kill them as if the unborn child were merely a bothersome glob of unwanted tissue. From these few examples we should see the glaring importance of regarding the Holy Spirit as a personal being.

He walks with us daily as our closest friend. Paul warns us in Ephesians 4:30 not to grieve this dear friend. In other words, we must give him loving, personal attention as we would anyone with whom we wish to maintain a loving relationship. This provides us a deeper appreciation that He is the Lord and giver of life.

God lovingly works in us by the Holy Spirit in a personal and gentle manner. What a blessing to have the Holy Spirit of God abiding with us! What an appropriate manifestation of the love of God. This is how we experience the mercy of Christ's gentle love. God has the authority and power to overwhelm us with His might. He makes the ocean waves to cease and the mighty winds to stop blowing. Yet He comes to us in the gentle breath of the Holy Spirit working from the inside out. He does not overwhelm us with might and violence, for His coming is altogether of a different kind. Cyril of Jerusalem was right in saying,

> His coming is gentle. Our perception of him is fragrant; his burden is very easy to bear; beams of light shine out with his coming. He comes with the compassion of a true Guardian, for he comes to save and to heal, to teach, to admonish, to strengthen, to exhort, to enlighten the mind.[2]

When we study the doctrine of the Spirit, we should never lose the warmth and beauty of the Holy Spirit in the various mazes of theological discussions. What a profoundly different way of persuasion than that of sinful men! Christians have not become converted at the edge of the sword as in other major

2. Quoted in Torrance, *Trinitarian Faith*, 228.

religions. They have not been cowered at the brunt end of a bloody club. We are not subjected brutally or against our will to the external authority of a given revelation. Rather, gently through the work of the Holy Spirit, we are persuaded and enabled to embrace the light burden of Jesus Christ as He is freely offered to us in the gospel. "What wondrous love is this?" says the Christian. What could be the Christian's response to this but love!

STUDY QUESTIONS

1. How does the doctrine of the Holy Spirit help in liturgy and worship?
2. What are two good images of the Holy Spirit?
3. When was the creed's section on the Holy Spirit expanded?
4. How did ancient notions differ from the personal teachings about the Holy Spirit?
5. From what can't the Holy Spirit be detached?
6. How is the Holy Spirit the same as the Father and the Son and how is the Spirit different?
7. How does the Holy Spirit function in a self-diminishing way?
8. What is regeneration?
9. What are the different ways the Holy Spirit helps us in our lives?
10. How does the Holy Spirit win us to Christ?
11. Find some Bible passages not cited in the chapter that are relevant to these issues.

13 Filioque

Who proceeds from the Father and the Son . . .

The Latin word *filioque* simply means "and the Son." It is a very small phrase that has spawned a very big controversy. One author says,

> This short statement has generated more controversy among Christians of the past than any other part of the creed and was one of the causes—at least, one of the explicit causes—of the schism between Catholic and Orthodox Christians. . . . Its ability to create controversy is the more remarkable, since few Christians today have any idea what it means, or why anyone would care about it.[1]

The phrase did not originate at the Council of Nicea in 325 nor at the corresponding Council of Constantinople in 381, which republished the Nicene formulation. This historical footnote is in some ways the nub of the controversy. The *filioque* seems to have been officially added at the Third Council of Toledo in 589. This council was not an ecumenical council, and thus it did not properly represent the interest of the church as a catholic or universal body. Since the creed belongs to the whole church, no single region (in this case the Latin-speaking regions) or no small part of the church has the right to alter it without the consent of the other regions. Consequently, many Orthodox Christians argue that the phrase has no legitimate

---

1. Luke Timothy Johnson, *The Creed: What Christians Believe and Why it Matters* (New York: Doubleday, 2003), 228.

standing in the Nicene Creed because it does not have binding authority as coming from an ecumenical council.

It doesn't appear that the council in Spain had anything but noble intentions when they added the phrase. They were fighting false teachings that seemed to remain strong among the Visigoths of that region. One author notes, "It was accepted in good faith as an expression of the Nicene faith and did not become an issue until the time of Charlemagne, almost two centuries later."[2] When it did arise as a controversy, it was cloaked in all the typical trappings of political maneuvering and intrigue. This of course added to the growing tensions surrounding this tiny but increasingly annoying little phrase.

Charlemagne appears to have made this phrase something of a personal cause. Like Constantine before him, Charlemagne wanted a unified church. He did not appreciate the differences he found between the liturgy of the West and that of the East. Other issues such as the use of icons were swirling around the atmosphere, charging it with all the components of a nasty theological/political thunderstorm. Charlemagne attempted to persuade Leo III to insert the *filioque* in the creed, but he was unsuccessful. Ordering councils and urging bishops to issue proclamations, Charlemagne did his best to force the word upon the Latin and Greek church. Still, it appears that the great emperor's interest in this word had less to do with straining at theological gnats as with forcing liturgical and ecclesiastical uniformity.

Charlemagne died before the controversy was settled. The dispute, though, did not die with Charlemagne. Time did not cure this ill. In fact, the division over this niggling little theological phrase only deepened with time. The rift was widened with the life and work of a man named Photius, the patriarch of Constantinople, in the late ninth century. He defended the historical supremacy of the original formulation and denounced western ministers who used the *filioque* in their liturgy.

2. Berard Marthaler, *The Creed: The Apostolic Faith in Contemporary Theology* (Mystic, Ct.: Twenty-Third Publications, 2004), 249.

One specific fight broke out as Latin missionaries competed with Greek ministers over the allegiance of a Bulgarian king. The fires of controversy were soon stoked and were burning brightly again. In order to emphasis their differences, it appears that the Latin missionaries pointedly used the *filioque* when they cited the creed in their liturgy. Both sides criticized the other over this scene. Soon the Bishop of Rome, Nicholas, was furious with Photius and both men found themselves issuing mutual denunciations of ignorance and error. The West hurled accusations towards the East, and the East hurled denunciations back towards the West. Theological and personal mud-slinging became the norm as this little word constantly sneaked its way into the mix.

Rome and Constantinople were growing increasingly apart politically and theologically. For historians, it is very hard to untangle the political from the theological dividing lines, but one thing is certain: the *filioque* kept emerging as a clear point of demarcation between both sides. In the days of Benedict VIII, who was bishop of Rome from 1012–1024, the creed was introduced into the liturgy including the use of the *filioque*. The Emperor Henry II pressured all the Latin churches to use the creed with the *filioque* in public worship. Because there was no controversy or interest in the practice during the Reformation, its survival in the western churches explains why many Protestant churches include the *filioque* as part of the creed.

The division between the East and West came to something of an official level in the year 1054 when the patriarchate of Constantinople, Michael Cerularius (1043–1058), disputed the role of the Bishop of Rome, Leo IX (1049–1054). Cerularius directly challenged the bishop of Rome's right to alter the words of an ecumenical creed. Thus, the disagreement was perhaps as closely related to ecclesiastical power as it was to the procession of the Holy Spirit. As their dispute reached a boiling point, each man hurled condemnations at the other. Again the West launched denunciations towards the East, and the East fired excommunications towards the West. In July of

1054, a synod for the church of the East officially condemned the Bishop of Rome, which included a clear repudiation of the *filioque*.

What in the world was the big deal? To the average person this controversy looks like the proverbial tempest in a teapot. Why did this little word cause such strife? As noted earlier, there were many cultural, political, and historical factors that worsened the controversy.

But why is this word important theologically? The word is an attempt to explain the relationship of the Holy Spirit to the other two persons of the Trinity. Does the Holy Spirit proceed from the Father or the Son or both? John's gospel became something of a focus for this controversy. Both sides rushed to quote the gospel, which appeared to muster support for their position.

John 15:26–27 in particular was a text of contention: "But when the Helper comes, whom I shall send to you from the Father, the Spirit of truth who proceeds from the Father, He will testify of Me. And you also will bear witness, because you have been with Me from the beginning."

Here we have the text from which the original creed borrows its language: ". . . who proceeds from the Father." The original creed does, in fact, essentially quote from this verse. The Father is the person of the Trinity who "sends" the Spirit, not the Son. This would appear to be a clear case. However, the relationship of the Holy Spirit to the Son is also defined as being conditioned by and through the work of Jesus. This is what seems to be stated in Acts 2:33: "Therefore being exalted to the right hand of God, and having received from the Father the promise of the Holy Spirit, He poured out this which you now see and hear."

The Holy Spirit proceeds from the Father, yet this passage tells us that the gift of the Holy Spirit to the people of God would seem to proceed from the Father and the Son. Thus, both sides were able to marshal evidence from the Bible that seemed to support their position.

The difference would seem to be one of ontology versus economy. Ontology deals with the essence of God as the divine being; economy deals with the actual activity of God as the divine being. The Spirit does in fact proceed from the Father and the Son regarding His economy or activity in redemption. We read clearly that the Spirit's work is intimately and irrevocably conditioned by and related to the redeeming work of Jesus. One author notes, "It is the Father who sends the Spirit, but the Spirit's coming is conditioned by and is in the most intimate connection with the person of Jesus and the completion of his work in his death and resurrection."[3]

It appears that each expression is not mutually exclusive, and therefore we don't find an explicit contradiction. Each one does, however, express a valid difference in emphasis. The original emphasizes the ontological relationship of the Father to the Spirit, while the *filioque* emphasizes the economical relationship of the Father to the Spirit.

Each position offers a helpful perspective on Trinitarian theology. The French theologian Theodore de Regnon has stated, "The Latin theologian says: three persons in one God, whereas the Greek says, one God in three persons."[4] The West emphasized the unity of the divine essence, then from there they struggled to explain how the persons of the Trinity differ among themselves. The Greeks, on the other hand, took as their point of departure the differentiation of the persons and then they struggled to explain how the persons of the Trinity function together in perfect unity. One can see that an added emphasis is not necessarily a contradiction.

There are far deeper theological and philosophical connections to each side's position, but overall they seem to reflect more of an emphasis than a contradiction. Though not a tempest in a teapot, the *filioque* or lack of it should also not delin-

---

3. Thomas Smail, "The Holy Spirit in the Holy Trinity," from Christopher R. Seitz, ed., *Nicene Christianity: The Future for a New Ecumenism* (Grand Rapids: Brazos Press, 2001), 155.
4. Quote from ibid., 254.

eate between orthodoxy and heresy. It appears that this may be a point of difference that both sides could tolerate without any compromise to principled, trinitarian orthodoxy.

The East, however, does have the historical authority of ecumenical councils on their side. If the church's creeds are to be announced and subsequently developed as a work of the whole church, then only properly constituted ecumenical councils would be legitimate for such pronouncements. Since the Nicene/Constantinopolitan Creed was the work of ecumenical councils, its work should not be changed without similar ecumenical consent. Thus, regarding historical or ecclesiastical arguments, it would seem that the East stands on firmer ground. Still, the point of controversy should remain something of a rarified point of theological difference, not a point of condemnation.

Study Questions

1. What does the word *filioque* mean?
2. When was the *filioque* officially added to the Nicene Creed?
3. Why is this controversial?
4. Why did the regional council originally add this phrase?
5. What great political leader tried to force the whole church to use the *filioque*?
6. How did this phrase fit into growing tensions between the East and the West?
7. What happened in 1054?
8. What was a major biblical text of contention?
9. Why aren't the two positions mutually exclusive?
10. Find some Bible passages not cited in the chapter that are relevant to these issues.

14 Who Has Spoken by the Prophets

Who with the Father and the Son is worshipped and glorified, who has spoken through the prophets.

Certainly by now, anyone who studies the Nicene Creed will recognize the liturgical beauty of this grand confession. If one thing needs repeating, it is this: the creed is not a recitation of dry theological information. The confession staggers us as it reminds us that we worship and glorify the only true God. Thus a raw or bare statement of theological data simply can't capture the confession of the true believer. We don't just verbalize a group of words; we praise God and we adore Him. Like the Psalmist, we are glad when someone tells us it is time to go to the house of the Lord to speak to him and to hear His voice. His voice is the voice of comfort and of peace. His voice brings healing to the wounded soul and rest to the weary. Therefore, when we come to the section of the creed which tells us that the Holy Spirit "has spoken by the prophets," we respond with warm hearts and are encouraged when we meditate on what this means.

Here we find a true comfort from the Holy Spirit, whom Jesus calls the Comforter. We receive consolation from the word of God because it comes to us through the Comforter. The authors of the creed knew that the words of God have come to His people in many ways throughout redemptive history. Yet of all the ways, the most common and the clearest means by which we have heard God's voice is through the prophets.

The fathers knew that God's wonderful way of revealing Himself was neither overly mechanical nor overly mystical and unclear. God used men in the past to speak to us. Yet, because men sometimes tend to speak their own words rather than God, the Holy Spirit spoke through them. God breathed His words from His own mouth using the holy prophets as His mouthpiece. This is a beautiful process whereby God artistically uses the personality, wit, humor and experiences of actual men, but He does so in such a way as to communicate His words and His words only. Speaking according to this same paradigm, Peter gives us the primitive expression from which the fathers formulated the words of the creed: "Knowing this first, that no prophecy of Scripture is of any private interpretation, for prophecy never came by the will of man, but holy men of God spoke as they were moved by the Holy Spirit" (2 Pet. 1:20–21).

The role of the prophet as the mouthpiece of God is central to the whole biblical concept of prophecy. We are told for instance that Nahum the prophet had a "burden" or vision. He had a prophecy from the Lord. The word *burden* is connected to the idea of an oracle or prophecy. The word *vision* communicates the idea of a revelation from God. This is not the vision of a dreamy, half-conscious prophet who is staggering in a trance. This is the revelatory word from God. We sometimes think of a vision as something like a foggy dream. However, the word for vision in Hebrew has more to do with an intelligible word from God. One of the best ways for us to understand this word is to see its use in Proverbs 29:18: "Where there is no revelation [vision], the people cast off restraint [perish]; but happy is he who keeps the law."

When I was a child, I remember this verse being used as the motivation behind a Sunday school bus ministry. I was led to believe that if we only had a "vision," we could accomplish what we wanted. The verse was used more as a positive thinking, inspirational message than as a focus on God's words.

The word *vision* actually means a revelatory word from God. Proverbs 29:18 helps us understand this because the word is used as part of a Hebrew parallelism. This means that the second part of the verse restates the truth, in this case in an opposite manner. We know then that *vision* means the word of God. This is not an ecstatic, unintelligible vision, but an intelligible word from God.

This is in fact the biblical prophet's job. He was the mouthpiece of God who spoke to the people the covenant words of their covenant God; he spoke the very words of God. He did not always foretell of coming doom or predict the future. When we think of prophets and prophecies, we too often think only of the idea of foretelling the future. The most notable example is probably the famous "prophet" Nostradamus. He is supposed to have predicted many of the major events that have transpired to change the course of history. You have probably heard that he made predictions that correspond to the Kennedy assassination and so on. He is even supposed to have charted the events that would lead to the end of the world.

Today we are experiencing a massive campaign of horoscope-type prophets who (for a fee) will predict your future success or failure, especially in your business or your love life. There is a plethora of telephone prophets who speak with a Jamaican accent and who will predict your future (again for a fee). They claim to be able to forecast future events, but this is not the basic nature of a biblical prophet. Telling the future, though related, is not of the essence of biblical prophecy and prophets. Certainly biblical prophets told some events of the future, but they did much more.

Even though it is probably the popular notion, forecasting the future was not always at the center of pagan prophets, either. Instead, the prophets of antiquity were often seen as interpreters of the dark sayings of the gods. They spoke to people who wanted to know the meaning of mysterious visions, sayings, or riddles given by the gods. Perhaps the most famous were at the oracle of Delphi. The Greek prophets at Delphi would stand before the high priestess of Apollo, who was seated near the entrance of a cave where rocks emitted trance-inducing vapors. The high priestess of Apollo was apparently under the heavy influence of narcotics and she would utter what was thought to be the incomprehensible sayings of Apollo. Rather than speaking intelligible words to the people, Apollo was thought to have made noises through the oracle at Delphi.

These noises would be uttered to the prophets who would then "interpret" them to the people who had come from all over the world to hear the interpretation of the oracle of Delphi. For a small or sometimes not so small price, the prophets would interpret the utterances of the oracle to the interested pilgrims. For instance, some people wanted to know what to do about a coming financial or business decision. They wanted to know what course of action would be blessed by the gods. So the prophet of pagan culture was not so much concerned about predicting the future, but rather interpreting the will of the gods to the people. In both cases, however, the prophet was a messenger.

Biblical prophets were not given to narcotics, ecstatic excess, or wildness. They did not work themselves into any kind of a wild frenzy in order to see visions or hear from God. The biblical prophet was actually quite radically distinct from the pagan prophets. This we see in the almost humorous story of Elijah's confrontation with the wild pagan prophets of Baal on Mt. Carmel. These prophets were wild, self-mutilating pagans who danced, howled, and cut themselves into a fevered frenzy—all of which stood in stark contrast to Elijah's behavior.

> So they took the bull which was given them, and they prepared it, and called on the name of Baal from morning even till noon, saying, "O Baal, hear us!" But there was no voice; no one answered. Then they leaped about the altar which they had made. And so it was, at noon, that Elijah mocked them and said, "Cry aloud, for he is a god; either he is meditating, or he is busy, or he is on a journey, or perhaps he is sleeping and must be awakened." So they cried aloud, and

cut themselves, as was their custom, with knives and lances, until the blood gushed out on them. (1 Kgs. 18:26–28)

Here we see that the pagan prophets of Canaan danced, shouted, and mutilated themselves as part of the normal means by which they sought a hearing with their god.

The biblical prophet is set in contrast to the pagan prophets. The starkest contrast comes in the nature of the prophecies' origin. The pagan prophets had visions that originated with themselves, from self-induced frenzies or visions. The biblical prophets, on the other hand, had direct discourse with God through the Holy Spirit. This discourse is always marked out as an intelligible exchange between persons; not an ecstatic utterance or mysterious vision. This exchange occurs as God through the Holy Spirit comes to His prophet and speaks to him in an intelligible exchange. God offers an intelligible expression of His word, even putting His word in the mouth of the prophet. The prophet in turn brings it to God's people. The biblical prophet has God's word because God Himself, through the Holy Spirit, has spoken to and through him. The biblical prophet is the mouthpiece of God as the Holy Spirit speaks through him.

The call of Moses and Aaron gives us an example of how God understood the role of a prophet:

> Now you shall speak to him and put the words in his mouth. And I will be with your mouth and with his mouth, and I will teach you what you shall do. So he shall be your spokesman to the people. And he himself shall be as a mouth for you, and you shall be to him as God. (Exod. 4:15–16)

Aaron was to be Moses' prophet or mouthpiece. God explains the role of a prophet by way of analogy. Just as Aaron is to Moses, so the prophet of God is a mouthpiece for God to His people.

Another apt passage is Jeremiah 1:6–9:

Then said I: "Ah, Lord GOD! Behold, I cannot speak, for I am a youth." But the LORD said to me: "Do not say, 'I am a youth,' For you shall go to all to whom I send you, and whatever I command you, you shall speak. Do not be afraid of their faces, for I am with you to deliver you, says the LORD." Then the LORD put forth His hand and touched my mouth, and the LORD said to me: "Behold, I have put My words in your mouth."

After Jeremiah complains about his call (just as Moses had done), God tells him that He will put His words in his mouth. The biblical prophet is God's mouthpiece. He speaks the word of the Lord as the Lord works in him to do so. The prophet is defined by the function that he serves as the mouth of God. The prophet of God is always spoken of as having an intelligible exchange with God as a person. He needs no drugs and he does not need to cut or wound himself to be involved in this exchange. The Holy Spirit speaks to him and through him.

When the word of God comes through the prophet, both he and God's people are transformed by it. Indeed, the biblical prophet is a man who has a life-transforming experience with his God. Furthermore, his life-transforming experience, through the work of the Holy Spirit, becomes something for us to experience as well. Indeed, the biblical prophet and the word of God he communicates brings us face-to-face with God. A premiere example of this is the prophet Isaiah's experience that he communicates to us, providing us with the same experience as we enter into the holy presence of our God:

In the year that King Uzziah died, I saw the Lord sitting on a throne, high and lifted up, and the train of His robe filled the temple. Above it stood seraphim; each one had six wings: with two he covered his face, with two he covered his feet, and with two he flew. And one cried to another and said: "Holy, holy, holy is the LORD of hosts; the whole earth is full of His glory!" And the posts of the door were shaken by the voice of him who cried out, and the house was filled with smoke. So I said: "Woe is me, for I am undone!

Because I am a man of unclean lips, and I dwell in the midst of a people of unclean lips; for my eyes have seen the King, the LORD of hosts." Then one of the seraphim flew to me, having in his hand a live coal which he had taken with the tongs from the altar. And he touched my mouth with it, and said: "Behold, this has touched your lips; your iniquity is taken away, and your sin purged." Also I heard the voice of the Lord, saying: "Whom shall I send, and who will go for Us?" Then I said, "Here am I! Send me."

Isaiah is not merely defined in terms of "function." He is also defined by his experience with God in his call as a prophet. The prophet is not merely a mechanical mouthpiece; he is a transformed man as a result of his experience. His experience with God affects a life-altering change in the prophet, which as the Holy Spirit communicates this to us becomes a life-altering experience for us as well.

The Holy Spirit has been doing this for God's people from the beginning, and the Holy Spirit continues to speak to us today in the life-giving word of God. What a comfort and what a blessing to know that the same Holy Spirit who touched the overwhelmed lips of the prophet Isaiah is the same one who touches us today! The creed gives us a profound sense of roots and connection to the wondrous work of God in history and into the future. Here we find a great comfort in our confession: the Holy Spirit continues to do now what He has always done for His people. In the words of St. Basil, "All things thirsting for holiness turn to him; everything living in virtue never turns away from him. He waters them with His life-giving breath and helps them reach their proper fulfillment."[1]

STUDY QUESTIONS

1. Why should we respond to this section of the creed with warmth?

1. St. Basil the Great, *On the Holy Spirit* (New York: St. Vladimir's Seminary Press, 2001), 43.

2. Why did the fathers use the phrase "the prophets?"
3. Why are the prophets the "mouthpiece of God?"
4. How does 2 Peter 1:20 relate to this?
5. How has Proverbs 29:18 been misused? Why isn't this correct?
6. What is a popular notion of a prophet?
7. In classical thinking, what was one of the roles of a prophet?
8. What was commonly used to "induce" prophecies among pagans?
9. What is the origin of all non-biblical prophecies?
10. How is the biblical prophet brought into a "life-transforming" experience?
11. Is God continuing to do this today?
12. Find some Bible passages not cited in the chapter that are relevant to these issues.

15 One Church

We believe in one holy, catholic, and apostolic Church . . .

When we think of our confession of faith, most of us tend to associate the gospel confession with a belief in the Trinity. We also naturally gravitate toward including a belief in the Holy Spirit as the continuing work of the Jesus Christ in salvation. My instinct is to believe that few American Protestants and fewer still evangelical Protestants would readily include a belief in the church as part of their gospel confession.

To many Protestants, this portion of the creed seems believable, but not a vital part of their Christian confession. This way of thinking emphasizes that the gospel has to do almost exclusively with individual salvation, and the church is not essential to this individual experience. The church certainly plays a role, but it is not central. It is hard then in this context to imagine that the average evangelical Christian confesses the "church" as part of their life-and-death creed.

This is not intended to belittle evangelicals' ideas nor decry their emphasis on the individual as completely wrong. Still, we should note that such a mindset is a striking historical break with the confession of the earliest Christians and with the most ancient ecumenical creed of Nicea. Like it or not, many evangelical Protestants are at odds with the faith of our fathers at this point.

Speaking as a former member of exactly this kind of church, I can testify to a kind of ethos that is at best lukewarm to the necessity of the church as a vital part of our confession of faith.

Indeed, at times it appears that some evangelical Protestants are involved in what is sometimes identified as the "church-growth" movement, which has even displayed a downright hostility to the notion of an institutional church.

Recently I saw an advertisement for a conference at a local mega-church entitled, "Unlearning Church." The proud pamphlets boasted about the virtual death of old-fashioned church worship and prophesied the steady growth of a new multi-sensory experience that would replace outdated notions of the church. Indeed, the implication was that it would replace the church. The church was a kind of "old-fashioned" idea that would eventually be discarded for something more relevant.

There is even a growing trend among "church-growth" groups to name their churches anything but "church." You can see signs for the "Christian Life Center." You may also catch an advertisement for the "Community Christian Center" or the "Family Christian Campus." You will see a wide variety of titles, but actually using the word *church* is fading in popularity among some groups. Not only do they deliberately refuse to publicly acknowledge that they belong to this or that denomination, but they act as if they are ashamed to use the word *church* as part of their name at all. This marks a radical departure from the ancient creeds of Christianity.[1]

"Holy"

According to the Nicene Creed, we confess that the church is an essential part of what we believe as Christians. How can this be? First, the church is "holy." This is more than a little important. This indicates that the church is not a human institution that can be taken or left as we have need of it. The church is set apart by God. This is why it is part of our confession of faith. If the church were an optional addendum to the faith,

---

1. Again the author does not intend to be unduly critical or harsh towards evangelical Christianity. Indeed, most of the present criteria used to identify one as an "evangelical" would apply to the author. The author's present statements are meant primarily as historical notations.

then we could exclude it. However, neither the Bible nor the creed has a "take it or leave it" attitude about the church.

The word *holy* in the Bible generally means to be "set apart." God has set Christians apart by the work of the Holy Spirit and calling us into the church. The work of the Holy Spirit then is closely identified with the "holy" church. The Spirit of God is the one who awakens us to life. The Spirit of God regenerates us from death to life. Likewise, the Holy Spirit is the one who brings us into fellowship with God and with each other as members of His mystical body.

T. F. Torrance says correctly, "The one holy Church is thus as it were the complement of the one Holy Spirit."[2] This should animate and give a bit more life to what we confess every week as we recite the Nicene Creed statement about the church. We believe in the one holy catholic and apostolic church. Listen to Torrance again:

> It is then in the Holy Spirit that we have communion or koinonia in the mystery of Christ, and are made members of His Body. The personalizing incorporating activity of the Spirit creates, not only reciprocity between Christ and ourselves, but a community of reciprocity among ourselves which through the Spirit is rooted in and reflects the Trinitarian relations in God himself. [3]

The Spirit of God creates us and keeps us in fellowship with God and with each other as we are brought into union with Christ. The Spirit, we also confess, is the Lord and giver of life who with the Father and the Son together is worshiped and glorified.

To be holy in this sense is very much to be the unique creation of God. It should be beyond obvious then, that the church is not man's invention but the work of God. We are after all the saints, the holy ones. Why are we holy? Paul spent an enormous amount of effort to point to this work as the

2. T. F. Torrance, *The Trinitarian Faith,* 257.
3. Ibid., 250.

sovereign work of God. In Ephesians Paul argues that God pre-
destines His elect people to their status. God accomplishes this
as the Holy Spirit applies to His saints the accomplished work
of Jesus Christ.

We must think about our salvation aright. When we as individuals are made into new creatures in Christ, we are immediately brought into a new household and new nation. We
don't have a choice in the matter as far as the Scriptures define
it. Becoming a Christian means becoming part of the church.
Is this how you think?

We are a lot like Eve, created for a purpose. When she was
created, she was not created the first independent woman. She
was not smoking Virginia Slims in the Garden of Eden and
checking out Adam to see if he was the right guy for her. No,
she was created as his wife. By virtue of her creation she had no
choice—it was simply who she was, and this is how we also are
as Christians. By virtue of our new birth, we are members of a
new household and we are fellow citizens with one another.

Salvation is covenantal and corporate. The new man is immediately transferred into a new humanity. This is a new humanity that comes from all over the earth. Hence, this new
humanity is what our creed calls "catholic."

"Catholic"

The church is also catholic. The word *catholic* here in the
creed simply means "universal." It is important to note this.
The Greek word for church, *ekklesia*, means the "called out
ones." The ones whom God by His Spirit has called out of the
world—from all tribes, tongues and nations of the earth—and
into the community of the faithful. Thus the great commission
is essentially "catholic" because God says to make disciples of
"the nations." The holy church is not tribal but universal.

As my son Robert and I were looking for pictures of St. Je-
rome, a famous church father, we came across some interesting
pictures of Jesus. They were pictures of Jesus from a variety of
perspectives. We found one portraying Jesus as a black man. I

mean they had Jesus dressed in traditional Jewish clothes with an afro and fellow disciples who were also black men and women. This seems to be typical of all of our tendencies to paint Jesus after our own tribal image. The most common pictures of Jesus in America portray him as having a light complexion and long blond or reddish hair—yes, he is made to look like an American. Neither of these extremes is appropriate for a catholic church. Instead, they reflect our tribal tendencies as sinners. We naturally tend to see the church as a reflection of ourselves.

I will never forget the indelible impression it made on me when I traveled to the Philippines for a summer and experienced the "catholic" church for the first time. We came late to a Sunday morning worship meeting and the people were all standing and singing a very familiar tune. I felt a smile come to my face as we walked toward the church because I knew the tune and the hymn that they were singing. I was moved to tears, however, when I actually entered the church because although the tune was the same, they were singing it in Tagalog, the native tongue of most Filipinos. I felt an overwhelming sense of humility and awe that God's people were truly as the prophets described—coming from every tribe and tongue of every nation on the earth. What a glorious God! This is what we mean when we say that the church is catholic or universal.

Indeed, the church was formed at Pentecost as the antithesis and answer to Babel.

> Acts 2 is modeled on Genesis 10–11. Like Genesis 10, Acts 2 contains a "table of nations" (v. 9–11), and like Genesis 11, Acts 2 records a miracle of language. These parallels serve of course to highlight the contrast between Babel and Pentecost. While the diversity of tongues at Babel divided and disrupted the nations, the diversity of tongues at Pentecost had the opposite effect of joining all the nations into one people. The gift of the Spirit thus implies that all tribes

and tongues will confess Jesus as Lord; the outpouring of the Spirit is for the purpose of gathering the nations.[4]

The church is the divine remedy to racism and tribalism that continues to destroy and to divide peoples all over the earth. God has and is continuing to bring together the worst kinds of ethnic and racial rivals on earth. The Apostle Paul says that God has made them both into one. Speaking of Jews and Gentiles, they are both reconciled in one body by one Spirit and as such He has removed the hostility between them through Jesus Christ. Paul leaves us no doubt that the new unity we have in the church is the result of God's work through Jesus in creating a new humanity.

God once set aside for Himself a specific nation, Israel. This nation was to point forward to the coming of this very moment. Consequently, when the Messiah finally came, the temporary barriers that once separated Jews from Gentiles were torn down. There were once two kinds of people, Jews and Gentiles. Now there is a new humanity in Christ that makes both into one as members of the church.

As we are united to Jesus we become part of a new humanity. Notice the corporate and/or covenantal character of these images. We are not just saved as individuals; we are part of a new humanity. Thus Paul can say that Christ Himself is our peace. He brings us into peace with God and with others who are also brought into peace with God. Union with Christ brings us into union with each other as members of His household.

Indeed, in Ephesians 2:19, the apostle asserts that Gentiles are no longer "foreigners and aliens." The first word he uses means in general a foreigner or stranger to a nation who is allowed to be in that nation but doesn't live there. He is allowed to be there but has no rights except perhaps those he has by way of a treaty with his nation of origin. This person would be like a tourist who is merely traveling through the land.

---

4. Quoted in Peter J. Leithart, "The Blessing of Abraham," *Biblical Horizons* no. 115 (March 1999).

The next word is similar but different. This word can carry the idea of a resident alien. This person is allowed to live in the land but without any national rights. Instead of being a tourist, this foreigner has his green card as we call it. He is a resident foreigner who is legally allowed to live and work in the country but has no rights of citizenship. Both words essentially mean "a foreigner" with slight distinctions.

Paul teaches us something amazing about the church. He tells us that the church is comprised of fellow citizens. Not only do we have all the basic privileges of citizenship, but there is a deeper idea as well. We are not merely citizens, but we are fellow-citizens, which stresses the unity and peace we have with each other as saints. We are not simply citizens of the same nation; we are "fellow" citizens in Christ. He even goes further when he says that we are members of the household of God, the church.

Paul contrasts the idea of a foreigner with that of a citizen. We know that Paul benefited from being a Roman citizen on several occasions. There are profound benefits to being a citizen, which is especially true in places like America today. For instance, there were many foreigners who were arrested after 9/11 but who spent months in jail without ever being charged with a crime. This could not happen to a citizen. We have a constitutional right to a writ of *habeas corpus*, which means "produce the body." You can't simply throw someone in jail without charging them with a crime, which then starts the legal wheels rolling. The list of citizenship benefits could go on and on, but the basic point is that citizenship is a blessing.

The word contains a preposition that speaks of togetherness. It points to the sharing we have in all the blessings of being citizens of God's kingdom. This is part of what being a Christian means; it means sharing with each other the life we have in Christ.

The analogy of our own national citizenship is helpful, but unfortunately many of us don't always take the time to appreciate what it means to be a citizen of a nation that protects and defends liberty. In times of war, as fellow citizens we fight with and for each other. We lay down our lives on behalf of our fellow citizens. This is certainly how we act as citizens of our country; this is also how we should act as members of the catholic church.

Now as if there aren't enough images of who we are as the church, we see that we are members of the household of God. We not only share with each other the privileges of citizenship, but we are members of the same family. This is why we should think of each other as brothers and sisters in Christ. There seems to be two levels or a progression here. Gentiles in Christ were once foreigners but are now citizens. Second, they were once outcasts but are now members of the family of God.

The church has access to God. It was precisely this kind of access that the people of Babel sought when they built their temple-tower. This is our deepest longing as humans. We are created in God's image so that we not only desire but need access to God. The failure of Babel is reversed in the church.

> "Therefore wait for Me," says the Lord, "Until the day I rise up for plunder; My determination is to gather the nations to My assembly of kingdoms, to pour on them My indignation, all my fierce anger; all the earth shall be devoured with the fire of My jealousy. "For then I will restore to the peoples a pure language, that they all may call on the name of the Lord, to serve Him with one accord. From beyond the rivers of Ethiopia my worshipers, the daughter of My dispersed ones, shall bring My offering. (Zeph. 3:8–10)

What kind of church is God assembling for Himself? He is gathering unto Himself peoples from all over the world. All racial, national, and ethnic groups are gathered into the catholic church. Notice how this is described in Revelation 5:8–10:

> Now when He had taken the scroll, the four living creatures and the twenty-four elders fell down before the Lamb, each having a harp, and golden bowls full of incense, which are the prayers of the saints. And they sang a new song, saying:

"You are worthy to take the scroll, and to open its seals; for You were slain, and have redeemed us to God by Your blood out of every tribe and tongue and people and nation, and have made us kings and priests to our God; and we shall reign on the earth."

"Apostolic"

The church is also apostolic, as one theologian says, "because it is founded on the apostolic gospel and called to fulfill the apostolic mission."[5] The apostles were given the deposit of the gospel from Jesus Himself to take to the nations. The apostles were specially selected and uniquely, officially commissioned to be sent out to establish the church.

They were given a commission and the gospel to carry out this commission. They also passed on this same apostolic commission, and likewise the same apostolic gospel as the message of this call. The potent message handed to us by the apostles is that which continues to animate us. We treasure it, we guard it, we pass it on the next generation and to the nations. This is not a passive reception either: it involves, as we noted, *guarding* it. We must actively receive it, guard it, and pass it on to the next generation.

Since the church is set apart by the Holy Spirit, we must note that no other institution has special access to God but the church. Central to the message of the gospel is the related message that those who don't believe the gospel as given by the apostles have no access to God. You don't have access to God if you are a Muslim. You don't have access to God if you are a Buddhist. Neither do any others except those who believe the message of the apostles.

The church orients us and defines us as Christians. The apostolicity of the church forces us to appreciate the church as central to our vision of life and the future. The church and

5. Edmund P. Clowney, *The Church* (Downers Grove: InterVarsity Press, 1995), 72.

not our own interests are central to God's plan for history. Is it central to yours?

It is to us as the church, the community of believers, that has been given the charge of the apostles to carry on the work of Jesus. The deposit of faith once given to the apostles is ours to carry forward as the church. What a great mission! Does the church play the kind of central role in your life that our text demands? Do the images of the church as central to the gospel and as central to the life-giving message of the apostle's ring true to your heart? Is the church central to your life?

Study Questions

1. Why might some Protestants not associate the church with their creed?
2. Why is the word *church* no longer popular among some groups?
3. What does the word *holy* mean and how does it relate to the church?
4. How is the "holy" church the work of the Holy Spirit?
5. Becoming a Christian means becoming a part of what?
6. How does Eve's creation help us understand salvation and the church?
7. What does the word *catholic* mean?
8. What is the Greek word for church and what does it mean?
9. We tend to see the church as a reflection of what?
10. How does the church reverse Babel?
11. What is a fellow-citizen?
12. What does it mean to be a member of the household of God?
13. How is the church "apostolic?"
14. Who has access to God?
15. Find some Bible passages not cited in the chapter that are relevant to these issues.

16   One Baptism

We acknowledge one baptism for the forgiveness of sins.

When the average Christian is asked to describe the Great Commission and the gospel, he seldom mentions the sign of baptism as central to the Lord's great mission on earth. Christ, however, did make baptism a fundamental element of the Great Commission.

As part of the Great Commission, baptism connects our theology of salvation with our theology of the church. This is of course exactly what the fathers of Nicea did. Neither the Great Commission nor the Nicene Creed considers the work of God in salvation and redemption without the church. The church, then, should not consider her role in the Great Commission apart from the sign of baptism. It is central to the work of redemption and therefore to God's great mission here on earth.

Torrance says, "Through the pouring out of the Holy Spirit upon the Church, it was constituted the unique place where access to the Father through the Son was grounded in space and time among the nations of mankind."[1]

Biblically speaking, there is no Great Commission without the church. The church is the context in which the commission is to take place. We cannot overlook this because modern and postmodern times have emphasized individualism, which runs into direct conflict with Christianity. The Great Commission is not merely about going around the earth, getting a bunch of individuals saved from hell. The church is the context in which

---

1. T. F. Torrance, *The Trinitarian Faith*, 278.

the Great Commission is given and the church is the context in which the Great Commission is fulfilled.

In the Great Commission, the church was given the sign of baptism as part of this commission: "Go therefore, make disciples of the nations, baptizing them in the name of the Father, the Son and the Holy Spirit, teaching them whatsoever ever I have commanded." Baptism is central to the Great Commission. It is the sign of the ongoing apostolic mission of the church as the unique "place" of God. It is a sign of the unity of all God's people under the work of Christ and in the ongoing work of Christ through the Holy Spirit in time and in history.

The triune formula testifies to the triune character of the ongoing apostolic mission of the Christian as part of the church. The connectedness of the Christian, the church and ongoing mission is held together beautifully in baptism. We cannot miss this connection. Baptism demands certain things of those who would follow Christ.

Certainly baptism testifies to the need for unity. See Paul's words in Ephesians 4:1–6:

> I, therefore, the prisoner of the Lord, beseech you to walk worthy of the calling with which you were called, with all lowliness and gentleness, with longsuffering, bearing with one another in love, endeavoring to keep the unity of the Spirit in the bond of peace. There is one body and one Spirit, just as you were called in one hope of your calling; one Lord, one faith, one baptism; one God and Father of all, who is above all, and through all, and in you all.

Here Paul's main point is the unity we all share in Christ. The church is one and must act as one. We must learn to live with the unity and peace of the church in mind. The Holy Spirit works in each of us not merely so we can go about living our lives in peace with God, but also so we can live in unity and peace with our brothers and sisters in the church.

Baptism is a constant reminder of our calling and that this life is not about ourselves only. We belong to Jesus and not ourselves. Baptism calls us to live unto God and His calling. We live for His glory and the welfare of our neighbor.

Baptism calls us away from ourselves and unto the mission we have as members of His church. Our natural tendency is to be selfish, but baptism calls us away from the selfish way of living connected to our father Adam. Baptism calls us to the new way of living in the second Adam, Jesus. Selfishness would drive us apart, but the love of Christ draws us together. All of us are to seek unity and peace with each other as represented in our baptism.

Like the sign of circumcision in the Old Testament, baptism binds God's people together in a common sign. Those marked by this sign are said to belong to the Lord. They have a blessed and unique place among the peoples of the earth.

As we mentioned, the church has a unique place in the on-going mission of Christ. The church has been given the ordinances and instruments of grace to take to the needy world. This comes to a world that desperately needs to hear the gospel of forgiveness of sins which is represented and sealed in baptism.

Baptism then is a sign of the uniqueness of the way. Baptism signifies the only way for men to have their sins forgiven. There is no other way. Only through Christ are men's sins forgiven. Only through Jesus Christ are men reconciled with God. Baptism directs men to the unique and exclusive call of Jesus as the "way truth and life." No man comes to the Father except through the Son.

In our baptism we are identified with Christ. We are identified with Christ in that we share, sacrifice and suffer for one another like our Savior did. This is after all what our Savior did for us. This is the mission on which He sent His apostles and this is the ongoing mission of the church. We follow the pattern of our savior in love for the needy. We lay down our lives for one another and seek the best interest of our brothers and sisters. Baptism calls us to this because baptism calls us to the remission of sins with which we are identified.

What shall we say then? Shall we continue in sin that grace may abound? Certainly not! How shall we who died to sin live any longer in it? Or do you not know that as many of us as were baptized into Christ Jesus were baptized into His death? Therefore we were buried with Him through baptism into death, that just as Christ was raised from the dead by the glory of the Father, even so we also should walk in newness of life. For if we have been united together in the likeness of His death, certainly we also shall be in the likeness of His resurrection, knowing this, that our old man was crucified with Him, that the body of sin might be done away with, that we should no longer be slaves of sin. For he who has died has been freed from sin. Now if we died with Christ, we believe that we shall also live with Him, knowing that Christ, having been raised from the dead, dies no more. Death no longer has dominion over Him. For the death that He died, He died to sin once for all; but the life that He lives, He lives to God. Likewise you also, reckon yourselves to be dead indeed to sin, but alive to God in Christ Jesus our Lord. Therefore do not let sin reign in your mortal body, that you should obey it in its lusts. And do not present your members as instruments of unrighteousness to sin, but present yourselves to God as being alive from the dead, and your members as instruments of righteousness to God. For sin shall not have dominion over you, for you are not under law but under grace. (Rom. 6:1–14)

In baptism we have the cleansing sign of the forgiveness of sins. Here is the nub of many controversies. Here is also where it helps to return to the original or earlier versions of the creed.

In the earliest editions, for instance, we don't find a causal connection between the sign of baptism and the forgiveness of sins. This is not to say that we don't have an intimate connection between baptism and forgiveness. Rather, the creed in its original language does not teach that baptism per se is the cause of our forgiveness of sins. Still, the connection is clear and powerful. Baptism is the sign of our entry into the life of forgiveness of sins, and thus is powerfully connected to that forgiveness.

The earlier Greek and Latin editions of the creed do not use the preposition *for*. Almost all of the English translations of the creed read as follows: "one baptism *for* the forgiveness of sins" (emphasis mine). This is not as faithful to the original. The original might read something like this: "the baptism *into* forgiveness of sins."

The word *one* is not in the second version but is certainly implied by both the context of the series of statements as well as the original biblical words from Paul in Ephesians. In addition, the preposition *into* or *in* reveals that baptism is a sign of connection to the work of Christ as Romans 6 speaks of it. Here we have an intimate connection that cannot be ignored, but which does not amount to a causal connection. This is important since there are traditions which teach that baptism is the means or cause of our forgiveness of sins. This is simply not taught in the most ancient versions of the creed.

Baptism identifies and initiates one into the community of Christ. This is the community associated and identified as the community of saints whose sins are forgiven. It is precisely this forgiveness that Paul mentions in Romans 6 that calls us to live a holy life. Our baptism calls us to live a life that befits those whose sins have been forgiven, which is what baptism represents.

STUDY QUESTIONS

1. How is baptism a central part of the Great Commission?
2. How is baptism a sign of the ongoing apostolic work?
3. How does baptism point us to unity?
4. How does baptism relate to our calling?
5. How does baptism identify us with Christ?
6. Is baptism the "cause" of the forgiveness of sins?
7. How does baptism relate to the forgiveness of sins?
8. Find some Bible passages not cited in the chapter that are relevant to these issues.

17

The Life of the World to Come

We look for the resurrection of the dead, and the life of the world to come. Amen.

The Christian confession is ripe with hope. The conclusion of the Nicene Creed gives us a compelling call to live an optimistic life of faith in Christ. The Christian's hope is not an absurd or wistful longing for what "might be," and the Christian is not a deluded dreamer—rather, the Christian's hope is absolute. The believer's rock solid view of the future is founded on the historically objective resurrection of our Savior. Here the objective work of Jesus Christ is subjectively offered to His followers. Indeed, there is no hope in any other, for no one but Jesus has accomplished redemption and no one can.

Hope resounds from the life of Christians. The Apostle Paul's words are fitting when he said, "For me to live is Christ; to die is gain." This is a worldview that can never be defeated. This doesn't mean that the Christian will never face the pains that accompany life and death. The Christian, however, has an eternal perspective with which to face the severities of life and the agony of death. We all share lives filled with sorrow and strife, but the Christian's suffering will certainly yield to the hope of the resurrection. What a glorious way to live!

> Most assuredly, I say to you, the hour is coming, and now is, when the dead will hear the voice of the Son of God; and those who hear will live. For as the Father has life in Himself, so He has granted the Son to have life in Himself, and has given Him authority to execute judgment also, because He is the Son of Man. Do not marvel at this; for the hour

is coming in which all who are in the graves will hear His voice and come forth—those who have done good, to the resurrection of life, and those who have done evil, to the resurrection of condemnation. (Jn. 5:25–29)

In Christ, the Christian has the death curse of Adam taken away. Paul outlines this reversal in Romans 5:12–19:

Therefore, just as through one man sin entered the world, and death through sin, and thus death spread to all men, because all sinned. (. . . For if by the one man's offense death reigned through the one, much more those who receive abundance of grace and of the gift of righteousness will reign in life through the One, Jesus Christ.) Therefore, as through one man's offense judgment came to all men, resulting in condemnation, even so through one Man's righteous act the free gift came to all men, resulting in justification of life. For as by one man's disobedience many were made sinners, so also by one Man's obedience many will be made righteous.

Just as through one man sin entered the world and death through sin, even so through the one man, Jesus Christ, life comes to those who believe. Death, as Paul notes elsewhere, has lost its sting for the Christian.

This is vital to the whole of the Christian faith. Paul enunciates this in 1 Corinthians 15:12–22:

Now if Christ is preached that He has been raised from the dead, how do some among you say that there is no resurrection of the dead? But if there is no resurrection of the dead, then Christ is not risen. And if Christ is not risen, then our preaching is empty and your faith is also empty. Yes, and we are found false witnesses of God, because we have testified of God that He raised up Christ, whom He did not raise up—if in fact the dead do not rise. For if the dead do not rise, then Christ is not risen. And if Christ is not risen, your faith is futile; you are still in your sins! Then also those who have fallen asleep in Christ have perished. If in this life only we have hope in Christ, we are of all men the most pitiable. But now Christ is risen from the dead, and has become the firstfruits of those who have fallen asleep. For since by man came death, by Man also came the resurrection of the dead. For as in Adam all die, even so in Christ all shall be made alive.

The resurrection becomes a lynchpin of the faith—without it there is no faith. With it, however, the faith animates our present life with the hope of the future. This means that our doctrines about what theologians call "eschatology," or last things, are important. This means that, generally speaking, one's eschatology always mingles with how one lives. In other words, what you believe about the future always determines the way you live in the present.

The Nicene Creed specifically affirms the following statements about the future: Jesus will come again in glory to judge the living and the dead, His kingdom will have no end, there will be a resurrection of the dead, and there will be a life in the world to come. These truths animate the Christian worldview.

The Christian lives a life of hope and expectation because of the reality of Jesus' resurrection and what this means for everyone who believes. The fathers used a word that expresses this idea. Earlier in the creed, the fathers used words that express the idea of "believing" and "confessing." Here at the conclusion they employ a word that could be translated "expect." The Christian lives with the expectation of the resurrection of the dead and the life of the world to come.

Because of the objective work of Jesus Christ we expect a final resurrection and life eternal for all those who believe. The word they used also was a word used in the New Testament to speak of the coming one or the hope of the Messiah. When John the Baptist asked Jesus if He were the one or if we should "expect" another, he used this word.

The idea of a man who was "coming" is connected to this word. Jesus is the "coming one." He is the one predicted in the whole of the Old Testament. Likewise, the Christian has a coming life in the future because of what Jesus has done for him. This is the life to which we look forward and towards which we live. The future life brings eternal purpose to the present life here and now. The Nicene Creed connects the eternal with the present in an exciting way.

Christians look forward to an age that is coming. This is certainly true because Jesus Christ has been raised from the dead. Death may scare those outside of Christ's covenant community, but not the Christian. Death stands as a dark specter looming over every man. The shadow of death can't be outrun or tricked. Hence, the ever popular picture of death as a "grim reaper." Death's certain grip on the throat of all men also grips men's souls with fear. But death has no grip on the Christian and therefore the Christian doesn't live life with fear, but with hope. The resurrection dispels the fear of death.

The shadow of death provokes images of skulls, screams, and horror. We know that men spend the better part of their lives suppressing the certainty of death. Yet death will come. In this sense, the ubiquity of death actually heightens the hope of the resurrection.

Though he may limp through life crippled and badly wounded, the Christian has a bright hope. Our physical bodies eventually get battered by sin. Our physical frames waste away towards the inevitable end, which is death. We don't get physically stronger and fitter as we age. To the contrary, the effects of death not only linger with us but press more and more into our lives with every passing year. You can't escape death, but you can overcome it in Christ.

Jesus' resurrection gives to the Christian to a personal, bodily resurrection of his own. Christians therefore are not daunted by death. Indeed, they may even be inspired by the hope they will find in death. A powerful and virtually mesmerizing factor in Christian history has been the unwavering spirit of Christians in the face of death. Enemies of Christianity have been bewildered and frustrated with the hopeful resolve that Christians bring to their cause even when they face death. Imagine that torture and death are the final and most potent tools of your enemies! If so, then they have lost and you have won. This means that though the enemies of the faith kill and destroy with unrelenting zeal, the Christian faith triumphs.

The most powerful weapons in the arsenal of the enemy actually propel the Christian to the hope of glory. This means that Christianity faithfully practiced can never be defeated. What a resounding note of victory and hope! No matter what happens to the Christian in life or in death he has a sure and certain hope in the resurrection of Jesus. Because he knows how to die, he is the best at living. He echoes Paul in saying, "For me to live is Christ; to die is gain."

Study Questions

1. On what basis does the Christian live a life of hope?
2. How should what you believe about the future affect the way you live?
3. How does the Creed connect the eternal with the present?
4. Why doesn't death have a "grip" on the Christian?
5. How has this frustrated the enemies of Christianity?
6. How does Paul summarize this approach to life and death?
7. Find some Bible passages not cited in the chapter that are relevant to these issues.

18

Key Players and the Historical Context

Many Christians have revived their interest in the classical culture of ancient Rome, which was the historical setting into which Christ and Christianity were born. Those familiar with Christian traditions of Christmas can probably quote the words of Luke 2:1: "And it came to pass in those days that a decree went out from Caesar Augustus that all the world should be registered."

During the first century A.D., Rome provided the church with the cultural stability and security that allowed Christianity the chance to be heard. For example, the Apostle Paul's appeal to Caesar as a Roman citizen is probably the classic New Testament example of this kind of protection. It appears that early Roman provincial rulers and governors thought Christianity was a sect of Judaism. Thus the church enjoyed most of the first century as a protected religion.

After the destruction of Jerusalem in A.D. 70, both Jews and Christians came under intense, harsh persecution. For the next two centuries this persecution was widespread and in some cases came from the actions of the emperors themselves. History records that Christians were thrown to the lions, hacked to pieces in the Circus Maximus, or even burned alive for the entertainment of emperors. Christians were clearly singled out. Ironically, the intense persecution did not destroy the church but caused it to prosper. Unlike others who confronted the terror of a raging beast, Christians stood resolutely against the specter of death. Their calm demeanor and their steadfast resolve in the face of such fear began to open the hearts of fellow Romans to their faith. This was a noticeably different religion because not even death could frighten its followers.

At various times in her history, classical Rome had been ambivalent towards this odd little group, which was now growing like wildfire. However, with the rise of Constantine to the position of unrivaled ruler of Rome, the currents of persecution changed directions. Instead of emperors who deliberately sought to hurt the fledgling faith, Rome now had an emperor who was actually determined to assist it.

Constantine (a.d. 274–337)

If the classical world formed the broader context for the birth of Christianity, Flavius Valerius Aurelius Constantinus, or Constantine I, provided the narrower context in which the Nicene Creed was born. Constantine's rule provided the framework in which the two main thinkers, Arius and Athanasius, could battle out their differences. In fact, the battle between Arius and his followers and eventually Athanasius and the other orthodox teachers created the doctrinal resolution that we call the Nicene Creed. At Constantine's call, the historic council of Nicea was convened in a.d. 325. This is a vital year for church history.

Some revisionist historians argue that the men at Nicea were not consciously creating a universal standard of faith and practice. This fails to account for the council's demand that everyone must adhere to the council's decision under pain of anathema or curse. This hardly sounds like a group of men uncertain as to the binding character of their decisions. These same scholars also argue that the council had no precedent for the idea that such a meeting would legislate for the Church as a whole.[1] While Nicea was unique in many ways, it was not the first of its kind. It is fair to say that one would be hard pressed to find a single minister at the Council of Nicea who was un-

---

1. Lewis Ayres, *Nicaea and its Legacy: An Approach to Fourth-Century Trinitarian Theology,* Oxford Univ. Press, 2004), 87.

familiar with the first truly ecumenical council of Jerusalem chronicled in Acts 15.

To the contrary, they had a distinct sense of the overwhelming significance of their proceedings as members of the first ecumenical council since Acts 15. Since the days of the apostles

> there had never been any attempt to summon a general council of the whole church at which, at least in theory, the church in every part of the Roman Empire should be represented, and it was by far the greatest number of bishops ever gathered together up to then.[2]

Regarding Nicea, one historian quips, "as it had no precedent, so it has no equal in ecclesiastical history."[3] This may be a bit of an exaggeration, but it does capture something of the momentous character of the grand council that met at Nicea. There really had not been anything like it in all of post-apostolic church history.

The Council of Nicea was convened in the year 325 in the ancient city of Nicea (in present-day Turkey). It was the first ecumenical council of its kind partly because up to this point the Christian religion had come under intense persecution from the Roman government, but primarily also because now the church had Constantine's official support.

The Emperor Constantine was the key political figure at the Council of Nicea. Certainly Constantine's conversion to Christianity is one of the major turning points in western history. It was Constantine who cemented Christianity's place as the most important religion in the empire with the famous Edict of Milan in 313. The Edict of Milan made Christianity a legal religion. But the zealous Christian emperor eventually went even further. Soon Christianity would not only be a legal religion, but the primary religion of the empire.

2. Richard Hanson, *The Search for the Christian Doctrine of God: The Arian Controversy 318–381*, (T. & T. Clark, 1988), 152.

3. Dean Dudley, *History of the First Council of Nice* [sic]: *A World's Christian Convention, A.D. 325: With a Life of Constantine* (Boston: Dean Dudley & Co. Publishers, 1886), 30.

A series of edicts of 315, 316, 319, 321, and 323 completed the revolution. Christians were admitted to the offices of the State, both military and civil; the Christian clergy was exempted from all municipal burdens, as were the Pagan priests; the emancipation of Christian slaves was facilitated; Jews were forbidden to keep Christian slaves, etc. An edict of 321 ordered Sunday to be celebrated by cessation of all work in public. When Constantine became master of the whole empire, all these edicts were extended to the whole realm, and the Roman world more and more assumed the aspects of a Christian state.[4]

Constantine had fought hard battles to make his way to Rome as the unrivaled leader. His outnumbered armies had faced overwhelming odds. Still he remained undaunted and moved towards the central city. In 312, as he prepared for his final and perhaps most important battle at Milvian Bridge, he believed he received a vision of the sign of the cross. Hence, the famous phrase *in hoc signo vinces:* "in this sign you will conquer." Eusebius first mentions this tradition in his *De Vita Constantini.* Assured in the dream that he would conquer with this sign, his soldiers' weapons bore the symbols of Christianity. He won that battle and later he defeated his final enemy after years of struggle. Constantine eventually reigned as the unrivaled ruler of the Roman world and was declared "Augustus."

Constantine had defeated his military enemies, creating unity in his legions. The Christian church, on the other hand, was facing a challenge to its unity. He thus set about changing the course of history. Not the least of which was his desire to see the Christian religion a united one. His motto included the phrase, "one Lord, one faith, one church, one empire, one emperor." This would make Constantine one of the key players in setting the context for the council of Nicea.

4. Clemens Petersen, "Constantine the Great and His Sons," *A Religious Encyclopaedia or Dictionary of Biblical, Historical, Doctrinal, and Practical Theology,* ed. Philip Schaff, 3rd edition, vol. 1. (New York: Funk & Wagnalls, 1894), 546–547.

For centuries, historians argued that Constantine dominated, controlled, or at the very least manipulated the council to decide what he wanted them to decide. Hence there was a latent suspicion that the decisions of Nicea were less the true orthodox faith and more the expressions of men under political pressure. This simply does not comport with history. "It is," says one scholar, "going too far to think of him as dominating the debates of the Council, either for political or theological ends."[5] One needs only to look at the constant defiance of one man, Athanasius, to note that the church was hardly under the emperor's thumb. Indeed, almost immediately after the council finished its business, many bishops in the church (including some who had attended the council) began to question the council's rulings.

Constantine did support the rulings of Nicea. However, simply the fact that the emperor took the side of orthodoxy does not prove that he forced orthodoxy on the church. While the church as a whole was hardly of one mind, the eventual Nicene settlement remained secure even after Constantine was long gone—and this was not an easy feat. One need only glance at certain Christians' unflinching resolve to die for orthodoxy in spite of numerous emperors who came after Constantine and who asserted intense pressure against orthodoxy. The unyielding resolve of Athanasius, for instance, testifies against the idea that Nicea was simply the politically formulated creed of Constantine. This was not a politically manufactured creed; this was the confession of the faith of the Christian church.

The Issue

The Council of Nicea was called to face a challenge. As Christianity grew, her leaders faced several daunting challenges; not the least of which were some of the overwhelming pagan philosophies that confronted the central teachings of Christianity. One such challenge was aimed at the doctrines relating to the person and work of Jesus. At the risk of understatement,

---

5. Richard Hanson, *The Search for the Christian Doctrine of God*, 171.

this is fundamental. It is certainly not an exaggeration to say that the most important truth of Christianity revolves around the person of Jesus Christ. He came to earth as a man to take the place of man and provide a way of salvation for men. The major question naturally arose: If Jesus was a man, then how could He also be God?

Another side of the same coin is the question, "If Jesus is God, then how could He also be a man? What then was His relationship to God the Father?" This became one of the central questions of Nicea. Was Jesus the "same" as God the Father or was He "like" God the Father? One theologian puts it like this:

> The central place accorded to Jesus Christ in the faith of the church called for a clear answer to the question as to whether he was himself Lord and God or only a created intermediary between God and man. Where was the line of demarcation between God and the creature to be drawn, between God the Father and Jesus Christ, or between Jesus Christ the incarnate Son of God and the world? That was the basic question by the Nicene fathers, and they answered in their unqualified acknowledgment of the Deity of Jesus Christ as Lord and Savior.[6]

Constantine was determined to see this question answered and to lead the church through this challenge to a unity of the faith throughout the world. The challenge to unity had emerged in the city of Alexandria and began to focus almost entirely (whether rightly or wrongly) on a man named Arius.

ARIUS (A.D. 256–336)

One historian of this period notes wisely that "speaking of theological groups or parties is a descriptive move fraught with difficulty."[7] It is necessary, however, to speak with some measure of clarity in order to communicate what may have

6. T. F. Torrance, *The Trinitarian Faith*, 2–3.
7. Lewis Ayres, *Nicaea and its Legacy: An Approach to Fourth-Century Trinitarian Theology*, Oxford University Press, 2004, 13.

happened. Likewise, the people who lived in those days used certain kinds of descriptions that guide us in our study. Thus, the key player associated with this challenge to unity was Arius of Alexandria. Arius may well be one of the most famous heretics in church history. This infamous distinction derives from the heresy which bears his name, Arianism. Arianism represents the earliest and perhaps the greatest Trinitarian controversy of the fledgling church.

Arius' basic error hinged on his teaching that Jesus was less than fully divine. He insisted that God the Father and God the Son do not share the same essence or the same essential character as God. Since God the Father is eternal and God the Son is "begotten from the Father," then Jesus, though He is God, is not one and the same with God the Father as "eternal God." In fact, he said, Jesus is called the "only begotten" of the Father. Hence, "he must also be called a 'creature' (a created thing), inasmuch as he was generated from the non-existence."[8] God the Father is eternal and Christ was begotten from the Father. It seems rather simple to conclude that the Son of God is not eternal because there was a time when He did not exist. Some have said that Arius' followers marched in the streets of Alexandria chanting, "There was once when he was not." It may be hard for us to imagine that a mere theological/doctrinal issue sparked such fires of controversy, but the people of Alexandria were so energized that they not only marched in the streets but also marked the walls of the city with theological graffiti.[9]

Arius seemed to have been very well-loved by the people of his parish. Unlike his arch rival, Athanasius, he is described as a tall, lean man. He emerged from relative obscurity as a priest in Alexandria to become a world-famous representative of heretical teachings on the person and work of Christ. He was quite popular in the city of Alexandria, and as noted above, his

8. Stuart G. Hall, *Doctrine and Practice in the Early Church,* (William B. Eerdmans Publishing Co., 1991), 123.

9. Ibid., 124. See also, John Anthony McGuckin, "The Road to Nicaea," *Christian History Magazine*, Issue 85, Winter 2005, Vol. XXIV, No. 1, Page 18.

followers were fiercely loyal. He wrote and taught, but many of his writings have not survived the centuries intact. Providence, however, has preserved a few of his letters and only fragments of his writings. Most of what historians use as resources for Arius' teachings come from his rivals. Though perhaps distorted, it does appear that we can reasonably reconstruct the basics of his teachings, at least as they relate to the great controversy of Nicea.

Arius' ideas were defeated at Nicea, but his legacy would live for a long time after his death. Though the emperor actually forgave him not too long after the council, the church would struggle for decades—if not centuries—to defend against his teachings. We often tend to look back at history as if all that happened was a certainty, yet the triumph or defeat of Arius' ideas was not a certainty. In the end, however, Arius' ideas were defeated, and his reputation would sink into that of an enemy of the church as he was ultimately condemned and his teachings with him. Traditions of the church, though they differ slightly, record that Arius' demise was like that of Judas, who betrayed his Lord. Here is one example:

> On approaching the place called Constantine's Forum, where the column of porphyry is erected, a terror, arising from the consciousness of his wickedness, seized him, accompanied by a violent relaxation of the bowels. He therefore inquired whether there was a convenient place near, and, being directed to the back of Constantine's Forum, he hastened thither. Soon after, a faintness came over him, and, together with the evacuations, his bowels protruded, followed by a copious hemorrhage, and the descent of the smaller intestines. Moreover, portions of his spleen and liver were carried off in the effusion of blood, so that he almost immediately died.[10]

Like Judas, Arius' ignominious death became a noted place of horror for Christians. Church tradition has written a differ-

---

10. "Arius," in *A Religious Encyclopaedia*, ed. Philip Schaff, 139.

ent story for Arius' nemesis, the well-known Athanasius, whom his friends would call Athanasius the Great.

ATHANASIUS (A.D. 298–373)

As the question Jesus' identity loomed large at Nicea, one man emerged as the ultimate leader of the orthodox. This man was Athanasius. Though he was only a deacon when he attended the council of Nicea, his actions there and over the next several decades cemented his reputation as a major figure in the history of the church. Even after the council, many of the same bishops who had signed its creed appeared at other councils, often reversing their previous decisions according to the way the winds of power and influence were blowing. They found themselves less in a domain of monumental clarity and more in a swamp of confusing arguments and controversies that at times seemed to threaten the very continuity of the Christian church.[11] The man who undeniably led the church out of this swamp of confusion and into creedal and theological clarity was Athanasius. While the stories surrounding Arius' death are packed with shame and horror, church tradition surrounds Athanasius's life with ultimate triumph.

There is no doubt that Athanasius played the decisive role in the history of the Nicene formulation. Some historians write about him as a mean, underhanded villain, while others eulogize him as a saint. Still, even his most determined foes from the past and from the present cannot shake his hold over the shape of the history surrounding the Nicene Creed. In this sense, if you study the Nicene Creed, to some extent you must study the ideas of Athanasius.[12]

Athanasius was an unlikely hero for the faith. He didn't possess the requisite good looks or natural, physical qualities one might expect of a hero. In fact, his enemies ridiculed his

11. John Anthony McGuckin, "The Road to Nicaea," *Christian History Magazine* 24.1 (Winter 2005): 18.

12. For a good summary of the historiography surrounding Arius and Athanasius, see James T. Dennison, Jr., "Arius 'Orthodoxos'; Athanasius 'Politicus': The Rehabilitation of Arius and the Denigration of Athanasius," *Kerux Journal* 17.2: A5.

outward stature—or lack thereof. Some even mocked him as the "little black dwarf." Though small in physique, Athanasius was a giant in intellect, and with what would become known as almost god-like energy and stamina, he would outlive twelve Roman emperors.

He was not a major figure at the actual council though he did attend it. Nor did his later meteoric rise to prominence spawn from an aristocratic birth or noble ancestors. He apparently came from an obscure, humble family in Alexandria.[13] In fact, he went to the council merely as an assistant to Bishop Alexander of Alexandria. Though he was not the key player at the council itself, Athanasius would later emerge as the focus of almost all the energies of the friends and the foes of the Nicene formulation.

When Alexander of Alexandria died, Athanasius eventually replaced him as Bishop of Alexandria, and Athanasius's writings became famous throughout the Christian world after he wrote a life of St. Anthony. He also wrote many influential theological works including *De Incarnatione Verbi, De Virginitate, Oratio de Incarnatione,* and *Contra Arianos. Contra Arianos* in particular is very important regarding the definition of, and defense against, Arianism.

His unrelenting zeal to fight and his mastery of theology and churchmanship assured the creed's place in history. Athanasius fought to protect orthodoxy on all imaginable fronts, weathering political, religious, and personal attacks. Subsequent emperors exiled him, persecuted him, and threatened him. His fellow churchmen sullied his reputation, leveling false charges against him and using every conceivable tool of manipulation and pressure against him. In one instance, he was chased from the pulpit of his own church as imperial troops broke into the sanctuary to arrest him. Yet Athanasius was undaunted. God had grown and fortified this physically small man, who was barely over five feet in height, into a giant for the faith. Indeed,

13. Timothy D. Barnes, *Athanasius and Constantius: Theology and Politics in the Constantinian Empire,* (Cambridge, Mass.: Harvard Univ. Press, 1993), 10.

this "little black dwarf" became the man who almost single-handedly protected the Nicene formulation.

Convening the Council

It would appear that those present at the Council of Nicea were at least somewhat conscious of its potentially powerful place in history, despite the fact that some historians seem intent on diminishing the council's immediate importance. This simply doesn't comport with what little we know about the scene at Nicea. Wouldn't it be glorious if we could for a moment open the curtains of history and enter the meeting rooms of the ministers? Perhaps we could hear the nuances of the arguments and the tension of the debates. Even more amazing would be to have stood among the dazzled crowds as the great emperor Constantine entered the halls with his glittering jewels and colorfully flowing robes. This was a moment of historical awe. It was certainly a moment to remember and the council seemed to have had a true sense of its destiny. This was no ordinary council; this was a council convened by the most powerful emperor in the world and perhaps in all of Roman history.

Historians are not sure of the exact location of the actual meeting place, but it appears there were buildings specially erected for the moment. Whatever it was, it was an impressive place: "So it was that he summoned bishops to his private lakeside palace at Nicea."[14] After all, you could not simply host the greatest emperor on earth in a common location. Tradition points us to a vast marble hall enclosed with columns at the edge of a lake. Perhaps like many ancient columned porches, it was open to the glimmer of the sunlight and all the beauty that was fitting for a king.

According to Robert Payne, the marbled porch directed one's attention to the center of the hall where there was a

14. John Anthony McGuckin, "The Road to Nicaea," 18.

throne upon which sat a copy of the gospels.[15] At the other end of the hall was another throne for the emperor. This was a richly adorned throne carved in wood and elevated above the other unpainted seats of the bishops.

The following is an account of the emperor's arrival at the council:

> They waited expectantly. At last they heard the tramp of armed guards, and then some high officers of the court, themselves converted to Christianity, entered the hall to announce that the emperor was on his way. The bishops were standing. Soon an avant-courier was seen raising a torch, the signal that the emperor was about to enter, and then like children, these bishops from Syria and Cilicia, Arabia, Palestine, Egypt, Libya, Mesopotamia, Persia, Scythia, and Europe were hushed. Human majesty in the person of Constantinus Victor Augustus Maximus was about to appear before their eyes, and in the history of the world only Octavian, who had ruled the Roman Empire during the life of Christ, had ever reigned over so vast an empire. Constantine wore high-heeled scarlet buskins, a purple silk robe blazing with jewels and gold embroidery, and there were more jewels embedded in his diadem. He was then fifty-one but looked younger, enormously tall and vigorous, with a high color and a strange glitter in his fierce, lion-like eyes. He wore his hair long, but his beard was trimmed short. He had a thick heavy neck, and a curious way of holding his head back, so that it seemed not to be well set on the powerful shoulders, and there was about all his movements a remarkable casualness, so that when he strode, he gave the impression of someone dancing.[16]

Few men and women have experienced a scene so full of an obvious sense of destiny and historical import. The ministers were there for a purpose and it must have seemed that God Himself had reached down from heaven to mark out this mo-

15. See Robert Payne's *The Holy Fire: The Story of the Fathers of the Eastern Church* (London: Skefington, 1958), 102.
16. Ibid., 103.

ment on the map of history. This was truly a significant moment in history, and the men of Nicea not only knew it but acted accordingly.

> By Constantine's orders, 1,800 bishops were invited to attend the council. Messengers were sent to all parts of the empire with invitations. Each bishop was allowed to bring two presbyters and three slaves in his retinue; the services of the public post stations were offered free; from all corners of the empire the bishops descended upon Nicaea, crowding the public roads. It was not a good time for traveling. The eastern rivers were flooded with the rains of a late spring, and though the empire, stretching from Britain to the borders of Persia, was nominally at peace, there were marauding soldiers and bandits along the roads. Fewer than 400 bishops answered the imperial summons, but their numbers were swelled by a horde of attendant presbyters, deacons, subdeacons, and laymen. Most of the ecclesiastics came from the East.[17]

While most were from the East, the council was truly ecumenical and represented men from all walks of life. Bishops from the East who had suffered intense persecution arrived with the honor expected of men so tried and marked by their trials. One man, Paul, bishop of Mesopotamian Caesarea, had his hands scorched by flames. Paphnutius of Upper Egypt was famous for his ascetic life, and his right eye had been dug out and the sinews of his left leg were cut during the Diocletian persecution. There was more than one man at the council whose eyes had been gouged out for the sake of his Savior.

> There was James, bishop of Nisibis, who wore a coat of camel's hair, and from the island of Cyprus came Bishop Spyridion, a saintly shepherd who refused to give up tending sheep even when he was elevated to the episcopate. . . . Then there was John, bishop of Persia, from lands outside the empire, and from the unknown north came Theophilus the

17. Ibid., 103. See also Richard Hanson, *The Search for the Christian Doctrine of God*, 155.

Goth, a flaxen-haired Scythian from somewhere in Russia. This motley crowd of bishops represented varying traditions of Christianity. There were sharp-featured intellectuals, men of abstruse book learning, capable of splitting hairs by the yard. There were wise old hermits who had spent the previous year clothed in rough goat hair cloaks, living on roots and leaves. There were men so saintly that it was almost expected of them that they would perform miracles during the council. There were cantankerous men, and men riddled with heresies, and men who rode to Nicaea in hope of preferment from the hands of the emperor. There were men who came peacefully, intending only to observe and then report to their flock, and there were other men determined to wage war in the council chamber. Yet in the last instance, none of these bishops except Hosius of Cordova was to have any great and final effect upon the outcome of the conference. [18]

When the conference opened, the hush and splendor of the emperor's advent was quickly replaced with the clash of theological swords. Arms waved and angry accusations flew as the not-so-glorious churchmen grasped for each other's theological jugular vein. The men not only argued but chanted and sang their views. One historian noted that Arius burst into a long, sustained chant (having set his beliefs to music), thinking the emperor and others would listen more keenly to singing rather than mere disquisition. At times it seemed that the council would devolve into complete chaos.

When one side sang, sometimes the other side would close their eyes, cover their ears, and sing out loud like children in a playground dispute. There was yelling and singing in different languages about a variety of items. The council was filled with hard-hitting debate and vigorous reasoning. Yet somehow in the midst of all of this apparent chaos, the council was working slowly towards a conclusion. At times painfully, and almost al-

18. Payne, *The Holy Fire*, 104.

ways arduously, they made progress. The confession was slowly being forged in the kiln of heated debate.

The beauty of the Nicene Creed emerged from the not-so-beautiful Council of Nicea. To those of us who work in the earthy and visceral day-to-day work of the church, we see in this council the paradoxical way God continues to work in and through His church. God's bride, the church, is lovely because of how He works her towards her future beauty. Thanks be to God that He uses the wart-covered and weak instruments of humanity to accomplish His beautiful ends.

The council came to an end on July 25, A.D. 325. They had deliberated for nearly seven weeks on a variety of topics beyond the Arian heresy. An Arabic translation of the canons discussed at Nicea, found in the sixteenth century, shows that they debated on 84 subjects, ranging from the date of Easter (they set the day as the first Sunday, not coinciding with the Passover, after the first full moon following the vernal equinox) to determining whether the clergy could marry (the clergy were enjoined to marry before ordination, but not afterward), and the jurisdiction of metropolitan bishops. The topics ranged from the practical items such as the posture of prayer to bizarre topics such as voluntary castration.[19]

When all of the final speeches had been delivered, they prepared for the last banquet. Here, as at the beginning, the emperor sat in their midst. Constantine was covered with the purple, gold, and precious stones of his royalty, but he sat with them at a table. History reports that he was in good humor since he thought his council had brought religious unity that would now match the political unity of his empire.

He complimented Athanasius and gave presents to the bishops he favored. At one particularly poignant moment, the conqueror of the known world summoned the saintly Bishop Paphnutius, kissed his empty eye socket, and pressed his legs and arms to the paralyzed limbs of the beaten saint. Tradition notes that he was especially gentle to all the other bishops

19. Timothy D. Barnes, *Athanasius and Constantius*, 14.

who had suffered under the persecutions. Finally, the bishops went out through a line of imperial bodyguards with bared swords.[20] They were exhausted and most of them were rather badly bruised in spirit as they began the journey back to their local churches. This was hardly the end of the controversies. Rather, it was the beginning of a period of intense struggle that would last in some areas for more than a century longer. It is important to note that in 381, at another ecumenical council, the Council of Constantinople, the creed of Nicea was expanded to include a few statements about the Holy Spirit and the church. It was, however, reaffirmed as the orthodox faith.

The church of the fourth century was faced with some very tough and very real issues. Arius and his followers had asked some legitimate questions that almost begged to be answered, and they were not the kinds of questions that were restricted to an academic setting. The church was thus working out her theology in the midst of practical pastoral concerns, and indeed, the theologians who forged the creed were primarily pastors. For Athanasius and the other pastors at the council, knowledge of God was a religious and not an academic matter at all.[21] The people of God share in this knowledge as they live together as members of a redeemed community. Thus the church must be constantly vigilant in her pursuit and defense of the truth.

Athanasius and others remained steadfastly committed to the principle that God must be known from the revelation of Himself to us. All discussion of God, including the terms and analogies used, "must proceed from an appropriate sense of the divine nature."[22] The church can't say less and she certainly can't say more. This became a key, not only here in the Nicene Creed, but throughout the next generation of ecumenical creeds. There are a lot of things that we would like to know as human beings, but this is precisely the problem—we are

20. Payne, *The Holy Fire*, 111.
21. Alvyn Pettersen, *Athanasius* (Morehouse, 1995), 195.
22. Lewis Ayres, *Nicaea and its Legacy: An Approach to Fourth-Century Trinitarian Theology* (Oxford Univ. Press, 2004), 112.

only human beings. We are creatures whose very limitations demand a careful adherence to God's revelation and God's revelation alone. If God says something about Himself, then it is proper for us as His human beings to submit to this Word even if certain questions seem to remain unanswered.

This is not blind faith, nor is it walking in ignorance. It is proper and fitting for the creature to submit to the word of the creator. If God had to submit to the interrogation of the human mind, then it would reverse the creation order; people would be God. Our finite or limited capacity as creatures should call us to humility to God's revelation of Himself. This was something that drove Athanasius to a relentless pursuit of the truth. He was committed to a simple but powerful idea of saying what God says about Himself: nothing more and nothing less.

When we are faced with a mystery, our temptation is to fix what we can't seem to know. Rather than submitting to a limited kind of knowledge, we are tempted to pursue one of two approaches: first, we can solve the problem by subtracting what seems to cause the problem; or second, instead of subtracting we can add something new so that the problem is solved.

The church can do neither. The fathers of Nicea recognized that there are many times when we must simply say what God says and remain submissive to the reality that we can't know everything because we are not God. As creatures, we are fundamentally unable to know everything exhaustively, and consequently we will be left with mysteries of the faith. This may be as much the blessing of Nicea as the glorious Nicene Creed itself.

STUDY QUESTIONS

1. How was classical culture the context for Christianity?
2. Who is Constantine and why did he call the Council of Nicea?
3. What was the "issue" that caused the controversy?

4. Who was Arius and what did he teach that caused the controversy?
5. Who was Athanasius and what role did he play in the controversy?
6. Why were the fathers probably conscious of their place in history?
7. Describe the council of Nicea.

Further Reading

Ayers, Lewis. *Nicaea and Its Legacy: An Approach to Fourth-Century Trinitarian Theology.* Oxford University Press, 2004.

Ayers, Lewis and Gareth Jones, eds., *Christian Origins: Theology, Rhetoric and Community.* London: Routledge, 1998.

Barnes, Michel and Daniel H. Williams, eds., *Arianism after Arius.* T. & T. Clark, 1993.

Barnes, Timothy D., *Athanasius and Constantius: Theology and Politics in the Constantinian Empire.* Cambridge, Mass.: Harvard Univ. Press, 1993.

Bauer, Walter. *Orthodoxy and Heresy in Earliest Christianity.* Trans. and ed. by Robert A. Kraft et al. Philadelphia: Fortress Press, 1971 [1934].

Behr, John. *The Way to Nicaea: The Formation of Christian Theology*, vols. 1 and 2. St. Vladimir's Seminary Press, 2001 and 2004.

Bellah, Robert N., ed. *Habits of the Heart: Individualism and Commitment in American Life.* New York: Harper & Row.

Bultmann, Rudolf. "The New Testament and Mythology." *Kerygma and Myth*, ed. H.W. Bartsch, trans. Reginald Fuller. London: SPCK, 1954.

Christian History Magazine. Vol. XXIV, Issue 85 (Winter 2005), "Debating Divinity."

Coniaris, Anthony M. *Orthodoxy: A Creed For Today.* Minneapolis: Light and Life Publishing, 1972.

Davis, Leo Donald. *The First Seven Ecumenical Councils (325–787): Their History and Theology.* The Liturgical Press, 1983.

Dennison, James T. Jr. "Arius 'Orthodoxos'; Athanasius 'Politicus': The Rehabilitation of Arius and the Denigration of Athanasius." *Kerux Journal* 17.2.

Dudley, Dean. *History of the First Council of Nice: A World's Christian Convention, A.D. 325, With a Life of Constantine.* Boston: Dean Dudley & Co. Publishers, 1886.

Hall, Christopher A. *Learning Theology with the Church Fathers.* InterVarsity Press, 2002.

Hall, Stuart G. *Doctrine and Practice in the Early Church.* Eerdmans, 1991.

Hanson, Richard. *The Search for the Christian Doctrine of God: The Arian Controversy 318–381.* T. & T. Clark, 1988.

Harris, W. Hall III. *The Descent of Christ: Ephesians 4:7–11 and Traditional Hebrew Imagery.* Grand Rapids: Baker, 1998.

Hebblethwaite, Brian. *The Essence of Christianity.* London: SPCK, 1996.

Johnson, Luke Timothy. *The Creed: What Christians Believe and Why it Matters.* New York: Doubleday, 2003.

Kelly, J. N. D. *Early Christian Creeds.* 3rd edition. London: Longman, 1972.

Machen, J. Gresham. *Christianity and Liberalism.* Grand Rapids: Eerdmans, 1990 [1923].

Marthaler, Berard. *The Creed: The Apostolic Faith in Contemporary Theology.* Mystic, Conn.: Twenty-Third Publications, 2004.

Newman, John Henry. *The Arians of the Fourth Century.* Gracewing, 2001 [Univ. of Notre Dame Press, 1833].

Ngien, Dennis. *Apologetic for Filioque in Medieval Theology.* Paternoster, 2005.

Payne, Robert. *The Holy Fire: The Story of the Early Centuries of the Christian Churches in the Near East.* London: Skeffington, 1958.

Pearson, John. *An Exposition of the Creed.* London: George Bell and Sons, 1876.

Pelikan, Jaroslav. *Credo: Historical and Theological Guide to Creeds and Confessions of Faith in the Christian Tradition.* Yale Univ. Press, 2003.

Sanders, E. P., ed. *Jewish and Christian Self-Definition: The Shaping of Christianity in the Second and Third Centuries.* Fortress Press, 1980.

Schaff, Philip. *The Creeds of Christendom: With a History and Critical Notes*, Vol. 1, *The History of Creeds.* Grand Rapids: Baker, 1990 [Harper & Row, 1931].

Seitz, Christopher R., ed. *Nicene Christianity: The Future for a New Ecumenism.* Grand Rapids: Brazos Press, 2001.

Strimple, Robert B. *The Modern Search for the Real Jesus: An Introductory Survey of the Historical Roots of Gospels Criticism.* Presbyterian and Reformed, 1995.

Torrance, T. F. *The Trinitarian Faith: The Evangelical Theology of the Ancient Catholic Church.* Edinburgh: T & T Clark, 1988.

Williams, Rowan. *Arius: Heresy & Tradition.* Grand Rapids: Eerdmans, 2001.

Williams, D. H., ed. *The Free Church and the Early Church: Bridging the Historical and Theological Divide.* Grand Rapids: Eerdmans, 2002.

Willis, David. *Clues to the Nicene Creed: A Brief Outline of the Faith.* Grand Rapids: Eerdmans, 2005.

more on topic from Canon Press

Every time a pastor mounts the pulpit to preach, he is explaining to the congregation what he believes the Scriptures teach. He makes statements like, "I believe (*credo*) that this passage means . . ." or "We can summarize this portion of Scripture by . . ." Should the congregation reject his extra-biblical explanations and summaries with the slogan "no creed but Christ, no confession but the Bible"? No, of course not. We know the difference between the secondary authority of the pastor's words of explanation (his *credo*) and the primary authority of the Word of God. Similarly, but even more powerfully, the historic creeds provide us with not just one pastor's *credo* of what the Bible teaches, but the credo of the ancient, Medieval, and Reformation Church. How much more authority than a single pastor's sermon does the Apostles' Creed have as a summary of the apostolic faith.

It follows, then, that the Nicene and Apostles' Creeds are invested with all of the authority of almost two millennia of Church history. This authority is secondary and derived, to be sure. The Bible alone has primary and absolute authority. Nevertheless, secondary, derived authority is real authority.

THE LORD'S SERVICE
The Grace of Covenant Renewal Worship

Jeffrey J. Meyers

Ancient wisdom was tragic wisdom. It was the wisdom of the Stoic who had learned not to expect too much, who had adjusted himself to the grim realities of Murphy's Law, who realized that history, like the individual's life, was a sometimes slow, sometimes rapid but always inexorable progress toward death. Wisdom involved disciplining, chastening, and controlling hope, if not its surgical removal. Hope was a youthful and charming thing, but had to give way to the grim realism of age. "A joyful sage": it is an impossible description by ancient standards.

Against the classical nostalgia for a golden age lost and unlikely to be revived, the Bible, beginning with the prophets of Israel and continuing into the New Testament, holds out the promise of a future age of glory, peace, justice, and abundance. The last state is not worse than the first. In every way, the last state is superior to the first, and infinitely superior to the painful evils of the ages between first and last.

deep comedy

Trinity, Tragedy, & Hope in Western Literature

Peter J. Leithart

Miracles are stumbling blocks to the contemporary mind. Liberal scholars and theologians would like to revise the Bible by removing embarrassing stories of Jesus raising Lazarus from the dead or feeding five thousand people with five loaves of bread and two fish. But the "problem"—if that is the way we think of it—of biblical miracles goes much deeper. The incarnation of the Second Person of the Godhead is the central miracle of the Christian faith. Inseparably linked with it are the miracles of Jesus' virgin birth, His resurrection from the dead, and His ascension to the right hand of God. His crucifixion as a sacrifice for the sin of the world is so closely tied to the miracle of the resurrection that denial of the resurrection would nullify the biblical meaning of the cross. If miracles per se are the stumbling block, then no revision of the Christian narrative will be able to satisfy the objector. Miracles are not secondary to Christianity. Christianity is inescapably a religion of miracles, or, more properly, it is the religion of the miracle—the incarnation of God.

Trinity & Reality
An Introduction to the Christian Faith

Ralph A. Smith